· *Jongmyo jeryeak*

· *Jongmyo jeryeak*

The Royal Ancestral Shrine Ritual Music of Korea

UNESCO Intangible Cultural Heritage of Humanity Series

Publication by | Ministry of Culture, Sports and Tourism
Planning and Production by | Korean Traditional Performing Arts Foundation
Written by | Song Ji-won · Yi Suk-hi · Kim Young-suk
Translated by | Kim Myosin
Photo by | Ju Byeong-su

Published on December 31, 2012.

MINSOKWON Publishing Company
337-25 Daeheung-dong, Mapo-gu, Seoul, Korea

Registration: 18-1

Phone: (82-2) 804-3320 · 805-3320 · 806-3320
Fax: (82-2) 802-3346
E-mail: minsok1@chollian.net, minsok1@naver.com
Website: www.minsokwon.com

Publisher: Hong Ki-won

ISBN: 978-89-285-0396-4 93670
Price: 30,000 (won)

Printed in Korea.

Jongmyo jeryeak

The Royal Ancestral Shrine Ritual Music of Korea

UNESCO Intangible Cultural Heritage of Humanity Series

MINSOKWON

Preface

On December 6, 2012, Arirang made it onto the UNESCO Representative List of Intangible Cultural Heritage of Humanity at the 7th UNESCO Intangible Heritage Committee held in Paris, France. With this latest decision, Korea currently holds a total of 15 cultural assets registered as UNESCO's intangible cultural heritage items, along with Jongmyo jeryeak (Jongmyo royal ancestral Confucian memorial ceremony music), Gagok (Old Korean songs), Pansori (Song and narration performed by one singer accompanied by one drummer), and Cheoyongmu (Cheoyong shaman dance).

UNESCO's Intangible Cultural Heritage of Humanity Program started in 2001 with the aim of raising awareness and encouraging protection of those items of humanity's oral and intangible heritage which are in danger of extinction. UNESCO first selected 19 original and valued oral and intangible cultural assets for its list and continues to add until now.

This book is part of the Traditional Art Text Translation Support Program run by the Ministry of Culture, Sports and Tourism of Korea. It is a translation into English of part of the series of Important Intangible Cultural Properties of Korea, published by National Research Institute of Cultural Heritage of Korea. We hope this book will provide an essential resource for those who are interested in or wish to study the Korean traditional culture but have suffered from the lack of material until now. It also provides an opportunity to communicate something of the excellence of Korean traditional culture to a wider audience.

As the old saying in Korea goes, "to inherit tradition is a way of creation (法古創新)." We have to develop along new lines, be creative and seek to move in the right direction at all times. Intangible cultural heritage is a sign of community identity which is continuously re-created in the diverse social context and plays a key role in enhancing social unity. Thus, the contents of this book form a fitting introduction to the excellence of Korean traditional culture.

Besides the UNESCO's intangible cultural heritage properties, we will endeavor to propagate a variety of Korean traditional cultural contents throughout the world.

Thank you very much.

December, 2012
Minister of Culture, Sports and Tourism

Yoo Jinryong

Table of Contents

Table of Contents

Introduction to *Jongmyo jeryeak*

Introduction to *Jongmyo jeryeak*

1. The Meaning of *Jongmyo jeryeak*

In its broadest sense, *Jongmyo jeryeak* refers to the *ak* (樂), or ritual music–including instrumental music (*ak* 樂), song (*ga* 歌), and dance (*mu* 舞) –performed at the Jongmyo Shrine, where memorial tablets for the kings and queens of the Joseon Dynasty (1392–1910) are enshrined. During the Joseon period, the royal ancestral ritual was regarded as one of the *orye* (五禮, five national rituals), and was regularly practiced in Jeongjeon (the main shrine of Jongmyo), five times a year, within the first ten days of the first, fourth, seventh, and tenth months, and on *nab–il* (臘日, the third *miil* (未日)[1) after the winter solstice in the lunar calendar). In the first and seventh months of the lunar calendar, the ritual was also held in Yeongnyeongjeon (the sub–main shrine). Currently, the ritual is performed once a year on the first Sunday in May. *Jongmyo jeryeak* has been performed as a composite art form, combining instrumental music, song, and dance in a demonstration of singing with accompaniment at certain points, as well as dancing, all of which are considered to represent the good deeds of the kings.

The general meaning of "*ak*" incorporates instrumental music, song, and dance, which together convey the nature embodied by saints. According to Confucian music theory, these three factors are required in order to complete *ak*. Furthermore, *ak* displays its real value when it is used in rituals as a sacrifice to heaven, earth, and the ancestors, which reminds people of their existential foundations. This is the reason that the ancestral ritual uses the complete form of *ak*, with music, song, and dance.

The overall appearance of *ak · ga · mu* is realized in the configuration of the *deungga* (登歌, terrace ensemble), *heonga* (軒架, courtyard ensemble), and *ilmu* (佾舞, line dance), which together form *Jongmyo jeryeak*. The three factors–*deungga*, an ensemble performing on the terrace of the shrine; *heonga*, another ensemble located on the ground in the courtyard; and *ilmu*, dance performed between the two ensembles–reflect the Samjae philosophy (三才思想) of heaven, earth, and man as the principle elements of the cosmos in Confucianism. *Deungga* symbolizes heaven, while *heonga* represents the earth,

1) The day of the goat (the eighth day), according to the twelve earthly branches of the Chinese sexagenary cycle.

and *ilmu* between them is man or man's affairs. The *deungga* is located on the *dangsang* (堂上) or *sangwoldae* (上月臺, the high terrace), whereas *heonga*, symbolizing the earth, is set on the *dangha* (堂下) or *hawoldae* (下月臺, the courtyard ground). With *ilmu*, representing man, positioned between heaven and earth–between *dangsang* and *dangha*–the cosmic order of the three is realized through the staging of the performance. Within *ilmu* itself, there are two styles of dance : *munmu* (文舞, civil dance) and *mumu* (武舞, military dance), because all of the important affairs of man occur within these two categories. When *deungga*, *heonga*, and *ilmu* are performed together in the Jongmyo ancestral ritual, they testify that the meaning of the creation of *ak*, which the saint made by assembling the forms of heaven, earth, and nature, is well–realized, and *ak · ga · mu* becomes the cosmos itself. In this way, the music that the musicians perform becomes the sound of the cosmos.

Throughout the Joseon Dynasty, one of the principles regarding the instrumentation of the two ensembles was that they were to consist of *pareum* (八音, eight sounding materials) : metal (金), stone (石), string (絲), bamboo (竹), gourd (匏), earth (土), leather (革), and wood (木). *Pareum* represents all the sound–producing materials that come from nature. Historically, it was the norm that the musical instruments used in *Jongmyo jeryeak* represented all eight materials, although at certain periods after Imjinwaeran (壬辰倭亂, the Japanese invasion of Korea in 1592) and Byeongjahoran (丙子胡亂, the Manchus invasion of Korea in 1636), there were times when a complete *pareum* was not assembled. There even had been a period during which *Jongmyo jeryeak* was not practiced. However, according to *Gukjooryeui* (國朝五

Figure 1. *Deungga* ensemble as currently used in *Jongmyo jerye*

禮儀, *Code of Courtesy for the Five Rituals*) from the period of King Seongjong (r. 1469–1494) and *Chungwantonggo* (春官通考, *Code of Courtesy for All Rituals*) from the period of King Jeongjo (r. 1776–1800), the music was performed with a full set of *pareum* instruments.

The musical instruments used in *Jongmyo jeryeak* comprise instruments from *aak* (雅樂),[2] *dangak* (唐樂),[3] and *hyangak* (鄕樂, native Korean music). The current instrumentation of the *deungga* ensemble includes *pyeonjong*

2) *Aak* literally means "elegant music," and refers to sacrificial ritual music in which melodies from the sacrificial rites of Song China are performed.

3) *Dangak*, lit., "music of Tang China," refers not only to the Tang Chinese music imported during the Unified Silla and Goryeo periods, but also to the court music of Song China, excluding *aak*, the sacrificial ritual music.

Figure 2. *Heonga* ensemble as currently used in *Jongmyo jerye*

(bronze bell set), *pyeongyeong* (stone chime set), *banghyang* (iron chime set), *chuk* (wooden box with beater), *jeolgo* (barrel drum), *janggu* (hourglass drum), *eo* (tiger–shaped scraper), *dangpiri* (oboe as used in *dangak*), *daegeum* (large transverse flute), *haegeum* (two–string fiddle), *ajaeng* (bowed zither), and singers. The instrumentation for the *heonga* consists of *pyeonjong, pyeongyeong, banghyang, jingo* (large barrel drum), *eo, janggu, chuk, jing* (large gong), *taepyeongso* (conical oboe), *dangpiri, daegeum, haegeum,* and singers. Of these, the *aak* instruments are the *pyeonjong, pyeongyeong, chuk, eo, jeolgo,* and *jingo*; the *dangak* instruments are the *banghyang, janggu, dangpiri, haegeum, ajaeng,* and *taepyeongso*; and the *hyangak* instrument is the *daegeum*.

However, the current instrumentation of *Jongmyo jeryeak* shows a great difference from that used in the period of King Seongjong. According to *Gukjooryeui seorye* (國朝五禮儀序例, *Reference to the Code of Courtesy for the Five Rituals*), the instrumentation at that time included string instruments such as the *geomungo* (six–string zither), *gayageum* (twelve–string zither), *wolgeum* (moon–shaped lute), *dangbipa* (lute as used in *dangak*), and *hyangbipa* (lute as used in *hyangak*); wind instruments such as the *junggeum* (medium–sized transverse flute), *sogeum* (small–sized transverse flute), *saeng* (mouth organ), *hwa* (small mouth organ), *u* (large mouth organ), *hun* (ocarina), *ji* (transverse flute), *gwan* (pipe), *dangjeok* (flute as used in *dangak*), and *tungso* (vertical flute); and percussion instruments such as the *teukjong* (single bronze bell), *teukgyeong* (single stone chime), *gyobanggo* (suspended barrel drum), *nogo*

Figure 3. *Deungga* ensemble in live performance, 2008

(suspended drum set), and *nodo* (pellet drum set). In particular, the *nogo* and *nodo* were necessary for rituals devoted to human spirits. As shown above, differences from current instrumentation during the period of King Seongjong include the use of many string instruments, and a greater variety of wind and percussion instruments.

The mixture of *aak, dangak,* and *hyangak* instruments is used throughout the sections of the ancestral ritual, from beginning to end : *Yeongsinhuimun* in Yeongsin (welcoming spirits); *Jeonpyehuimun* in Jeonpye (gift offering); *Botaepyeong* and *munmu* in Choheon (the first wine offering); *Jeongdaeeop* and *mumu* in Aheon (the second wine offering), and Jongheon (the third wine offering); *Punganjiak* in Jinchan (food offering); *Eunganjiak* in Cheolbyeondu (removing the food offering); and *Heunganjiak* in Songsin (sending off the spirits).

Figure 4. *Heonga* ensemble in live performance, 2008

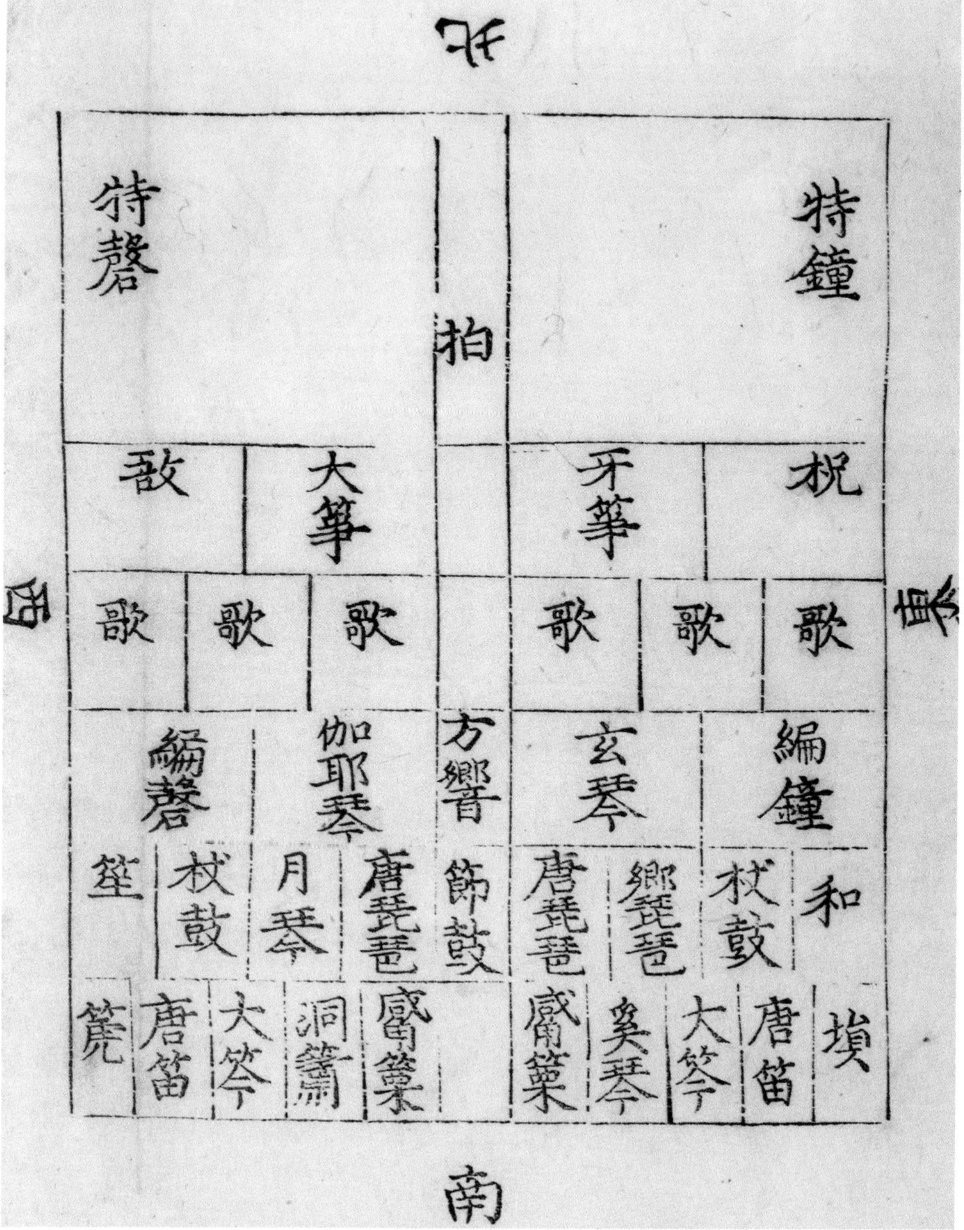

Figure 5. *Deungga* ensemble arrangement in *Gukjooryeui seorye*

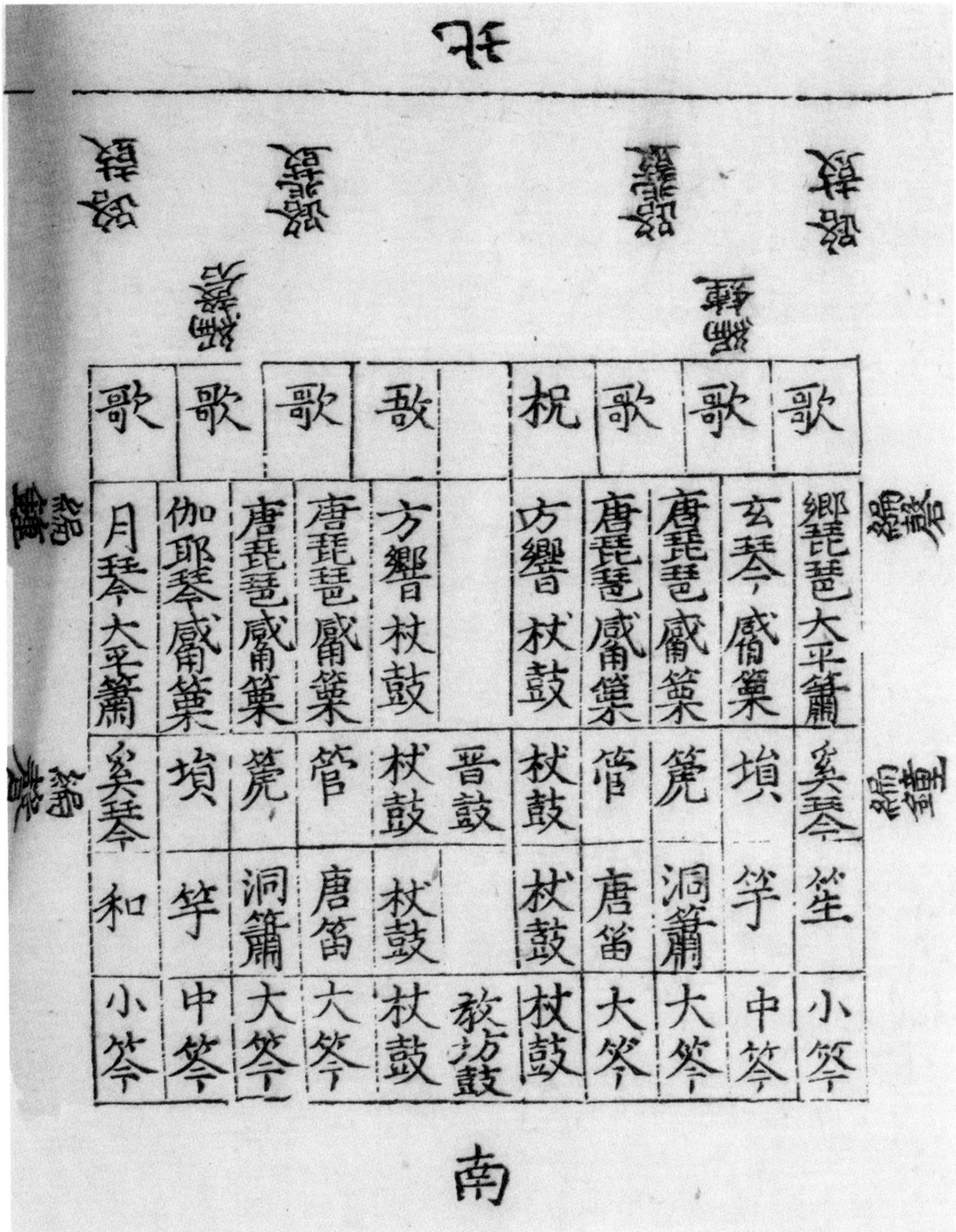

Figure 6. *Heonga* ensemble arrangement in *Gukjooryeui seorye*

Akjang (樂章, the texts or hymns sung in the ritual with instrumental accompaniment) contain texts praising the achievements of past kings. These are based on the idea that "when a king rises up, his music is certainly established, and after achieving meritorious deeds and political stability, great kings create music embodying the virtue of kings."[4] The use of the Chinese character "*seong*" (成, literally "achieve") to count musical pieces in *Jongmyo jeryeak* is related to paying respect to the kings' achievements.

Currently, *Jongmyo jeryeak* consists of the eleven pieces of *Botaepyeong*, praising kings' civil achievements and the eleven pieces of *Jeongdaeeop*, praising their military achievements. The eleven *Botaepyeong* pieces are "Huimun," "Gimyeong," "Gwiin," "Hyeongga," "Jimnyeong," "Yunghwa," "Hyeonmi," "Yonggwang–Jeongmyeong," "Junggwang," "Daeyu," and "Yeokseong." The eleven *Jeongdaeeop* pieces are "Somu," "Dokgyeong," "Takjeong," "Seonwi," "Sinjeong," "Bunung," "Suneung," "Chongyu," "Jeongse," "Hyeokjeong," and "Yeonggwan." *Botaepyeong* is performed during Yeongsin, Jeonpye, and Choheon, while *Jeongdaeeop* is performed in Aheon and Jongheon.

The dance performed in *Jongmyo jeryeak* is called *ilmu* (佾舞), or line dance; "*il*" (佾) refers to the formation of the dancers in lines. The number of lines differs, according to the status of the subject of the rite : *parilmu* (八佾舞, sixty-four dancers in eight lines) for an emperor; *yugilmu* (六佾舞, thirty–six dancers in six lines) for a feudal lord; *sailmu* (四佾舞, sixteen dancers in four lines) for a noble lord; and *iilmu* (二佾舞, four dancers in two lines) for a

4) *Jeungbomunheonbigo* Vol. 90 "Akgo" No. 1–"一王之興, 必有一王之樂… 古之聖王, 功成治定, 制爲聲樂, 皆各象其德."

Figure 7. *Munmu* (civil dance) with *yak* and *jeok*

Figure 8. *Mumu* (military dance) with *chang* and *geom*

scholar. During the Joseon Dynasty, *ilmu* was performed with thirty–six dancers in six lines, since the dynasty was considered to be a feudal kingdom of China. For civil dances, the dancers held a *yak* (籥, flute) in their left hand and a *jeok* (翟, dance implement made of pheasant feathers) in right hand. For military dances, the twelve dancers in the first two lines held a *geom* (劍, sword); the twelve dancers in the third and fourth lines held a *chang* (槍, spear), and the dancers in the last two lines held *gungsi* (弓矢, bow and arrow). However, after King Seongjong, the bow and arrow were disused, and the first three lines of dancers held swords while the rest used spears.

In 1897, as King Gojong proclaimed the founding of the Korean Empire and became its emperor, the *parilmu* was performed. Dancers in the first four lines held *mokgeom* (木劍, wooden swords) while dancers in the last four lines held *mokchang* (木槍, wooden spears). The names of the ensembles were also changed from *deungga* and *heonga* to *deungga* and *gungga* (宮架), which were names of ensembles used for an emperor. After Korean annexation by Japan in 1910, the status of the Yi dynasty was downgraded to that of a relative of the emperor of Japan; accordingly, the level of the ancestral ritual was also lowered, using *yugilmu*. After annexation, the ritual was performed intermittently until the liberation from Japan in 1945. From liberation to 1968, the ancestral ritual ceased. However, with the designation of *Jongmyo jeryeak* as the first National Important Intangible Cultural Heritage in 1964, and following five years of preparation for the reestablishment of the music, the performance was restored in 1969 with the *parilmu*.

Since 1971, *Jongmyo jerye* (the royal ancestral ritual) has been held

Figure 9 and Figure 10. *Munmu* (civil dance)

Figure 11 and Figure 12. *Mumu* (military dance)

annually without interruption by the Jeonju Lee Royal Family Members Foundation (Jeonju Yi Ssi Daedong Jongyagwon) on the first Sunday in May.

2. Understanding the Ritual Music through Treatises on Royal Ancestral Rituals

Jongmyo, the royal ancestral shrine, is located on the left side of Gyeongbok Palace (the king's palace), symmetrically with Sajikdan (the national altar to the gods of land and grain) which is located on the right side of the palace. The placement of the shrine on the eastern side and the altar on the western side of the city is based on writings in *Yegi* (禮記, Classic of Rites) which state that "the way of man heads toward *yang* (陽) and the way of the earth heads toward *eum* (陰), and the east is *yang* and the west is *eum*."[5)]

In the beginning of the Joseon Dynasty, the royal ancestral shrine was built on the site of the royal ancestral shrine of the Goryeo Dynasty, located in Gaeseong, the capital of Goryeo.[6)] After transferring the capital to Hanyang (present–day Seoul) in 1394, King Taejo decided to build a new ancestral shrine at Hunjeong-dong, the current location.[7)] In November of the same year, the king went to Yongsan–gang (the Yongsan area of the Han River) in person to examine lumber for the shrine building, and on December 4, he

5) Refer to the *Jeui* (祭儀) and *Gyoteuksaeng* (郊特牲) sections in *Yegi*.

6) *Taejo sillok* (*The Annals of King Taejo*) Vol. 2, articles from the first year of King Taejo's reign, on 30, September.

7) *Doseongji* (都城志) section in *Gunggwolji* (宮闕志) Vol. 5–'宗廟, "太祖三年甲戌始建"

observed the groundbreaking for the shrine. In 1395, King Taejo again made a royal visit to view the construction of Jongmyo; in September of the same year, the king established Iandogam (a special office charged with transferring the ancestral tablets), and appointed scholar–official Kwon Geun to be in charge of the task, sending him to Yuhusa (an office in Gaeseong) to transfer the royal ancestral tablets to the newly–built shrine in Seoul. On September 27 the same year, the king held a purification ceremony, and on the 28th, the ancestral tablets were relocated into the new shrine with a special ceremony celebrating the transfer. On October 5, the first *Jongmyo jerye* was performed in the new shrine.[8] In the first royal ancestral ritual, King Taejo served as the officiant in the first wine offering, the crown–prince was the officiant at the second offering, and Sim Sa-hyeng, the second vice–premier was officiant for the third offering.

At first, the *Jongmyo jerye* of the Joseon Dynasty strongly resembled the Goryeo Dynasty tradition. However, in 1430 (the twelfth year of King Sejong's reign), *Jongmyo jeryeak* was performed in a version rearranged by Pak Yeon. After 1464 (the tenth year of King Sejo's reign), *Botaepyeong* and *Jeongdaeeop* –which had been used as banquet music during King Sejong's time–became *Jongmyo jeryeak*. This music is the prototype of the current *Jongmyo jeryeak.*

In the *Gilrye* (吉禮, auspicious rites) section of *Gukjooryeui*, there are detailed explanations regarding the procedures of the *Jongmyo jerye* ritual,

8) *Taejo sillok* (*The Annals of King Taejo*) Vol. 6, the third year of King Taejo's reign, on 4, December; Vol. 8, the fourth year of King Taejo's reign, on 27, July; the same year, on 1, September (intercalary month); the same year, on 26, September (intercalary month); the same year, on 27, September (intercalary month); the same year, on 28, September (intercalary month); the same year, on 5, October.

describing everything from the preparations for the ritual to the period following completion of the ceremony. The book describes the ritual in lengthy detail, from Jaegye (齋戒, purification ceremony) held seven days prior to *Jongmyo jerye* to Chingha (稱賀, celebration for well–completion) that took place after the king's return to the palace. This extended delineation of the ritual is different from the general understanding of *Jongmyo jerye*, which only includes the steps from Yeongsin to Mangnyo (望燎, burning of the written prayers and sacrificial goods). In other words, from the perspective of the authors of *Gukjooryeui* the ritual begins even with the process of preparing for the ritual.

Strictly speaking, *Jongmyo jerye* begins with the purification ceremony that takes place seven days prior to the ritual. Three days before the ritual, Jinseol (陳設, setting of offering tables) begins, and one day prior to the ritual, there are Geogachulgung (車駕出宮, the king's procession from the palace to Jongmyo Shrine) and Seongsaenggi (省牲器, the procedure for examining sacrifices and utensils). On the ritual day, beginning with Singwan (晨祼, welcoming spirits at dawn) at daybreak, *Jongmyo jerye* is conducted in the order of Gwesik (饋食), Jinchan (進饌), Choheon (初獻), Aheon (亞獻), Jongheon (終獻), Eumboksujo (飮福受胙), Cheolbyeondu (徹籩豆), Mangye (望瘞, changed to Mangnyo since King Yeongjo (英祖, r. 1724–1776)), Geogahwangung (車駕還宮), and Chingha (稱賀).

Jaegye is a ceremony in which the participants of *Jongmyo jerye* purify their bodies and minds in order to devote themselves to the ritual. Because

Jongmyo jerye belongs to the category of Daesa (大祀, large–scale rituals), seven days of purification are required, consisting of four days of Sanjae (散齋) and three days of Chijae (致齋). During the Sanjae period, the appointed officiants were prohibited from condoling with mourners, visiting the sick, and listening to music. Furthermore, they were not allowed to sign criminal death documents, drink alcohol, eat spicy food, green onions, scallions, or garlic, and to be involved in any dirty or harmful affairs. During the Chijae period, officiants devoted themselves solely to matters related to the ritual. Musicians and dancers also conducted the purification process and stayed overnight at Yejo (禮曹, a branch of the administrative agency responsible for the ritual). They participated in the royal ancestral ritual after having attended the Iui (肄儀, learning the customary procedures of the ritual) gathering at Uijeongbu (議政府, the highest administrative agency) one day prior to the ritual.

In the following section, I examine the process of the ritual after the purification procedure, based on records in *Gukjooryeui* and *Gukjooryeui seorye*, especially focusing on procedures employing music and dance. In addition, I survey the preparations for the music and dance performances in order to comprehend the performance in the overall context of *Jongmyo jerye*.

[Jinseol (陳設)] Jinseol is a procedure to prepare all necessary goods for the ritual; preparations begin three days before the ceremony. Officials from Jeonseolsa (典設司, an office charged with the preparation of tents) set up *socha* (小次, a temporary tent for the king) and other tents for the crown prince, courtiers, officiants, and the royal family. Two days prior to the ritual, the person in charge of the Jongmyo Shrine cleans up inside and outside the shrine, and officials from Jeonseolsa set up a tent with drapery to store the sacrificial offerings. *Jeonak* (典樂, officials belonging to Jangakwon (掌樂院, the Royal Music Institute)) position the *deungga* ensemble on the center of the floor in front of the shrine and the *heonga* ensemble toward the north in the courtyard. One day before the ritual, the *jiprye* (執禮, an officiant in charge of reading *holgi* (笏記, the order of service)) installs the *panwi* (版位, a place for the king to stand) on the stairway on the eastern side of the shrine so the king faces the west, and sets up a place to eat the food offerings after completion of the ritual. In addition, places for officiants charged with the second and third wine offerings, and for *hyeomnyullang* (協律郎, officials in charge of the progress of musical performance) and *jeonak* are prepared. Also, the *mangyewi* (望瘞位, a place to view the burial of wooden prayer holders and general offerings) is set up. On the ritual day, before the beginning of the service, the *gungwiryeong* (宮闈令, an official in charge of ancestral tablets) opens the doors to each chamber, and arranges curtains, mats, and chests. In addition, he prepares incense burners, incense boxes, candlesticks, necessary utensils, wooden prayer holders, trays used for burning of the fur and blood of sacrifices, and hand basins for the king and other officiants.

[Geogachulgung (車駕出宮)] A procedure followed when the king leaves the palace in a royal carriage, Geogachulgung begins two days before *Jongmyo jerye* with the setting up of instruments for the *heonga* ensemble in the courtyard of Geunjeongjeon (the throne hall) in Gyeongbok Palace. However, these instruments are just for display, not for playing. One day before the ritual, a place is prepared for the crown prince to stand while escorting the king in front of the temporary tent outside Gwanghwamun (the main gate of Gyeongbok Palace). When a drum gives its first command, the royal procession is prepared in front of the middle gate of the palace, and the general officiants are ready in their court attire. When the drum signals a second time, royal guards arrive and stand in the courtyard. When the *pilseon* (弼善, an official in charge of educating the crown prince) reports the completion of preparations to the prince, the crown prince emerges from his room in his court dress and takes a position in the temporary tent. When the drum signals a third time, the crown prince emerges from the tent and moves to the place prepared for escorting the king. As preparations are completed, the king, dressed in his court attire and riding on a small palanquin, exits the throne hall and changes to a large palanquin, and the royal procession leaves the main gate of the palace. When the king's procession arrives at the gate of Jongmyo Shrine, the king moves from the large palanquin to a small palanquin, and enters the building.

[Seongsaenggi (省牲器)] Seongsaenggi is a procedure for examining the ritual utensils and sacrifices. One day prior to the ritual, the *jongheongwan* (終獻官, an officiant in charge of the third wine offering) and *daechuk*(大祝, an officiant in charge of reading the prayer) examine the sacrifices for their cleanliness and plumpness. *Jongheongwan* also visits the kitchen, examining the cauldron in which the sacrifice will be boiled, and supervises its washing. *Chanin* (贊引, an official in charge of supervising the order of the ritual) and *gamchal* (監察, an official overseeing the ritual) go to the kitchen and examine utensils. As the *jeonsagwan* (典祀官, an official charged with necessary chores for the ritual) and *jaein* (宰人, an official in charge of slaughtering the sacrifices) kill the sacrifices with a *nando* (鸞刀, a special knife used only for *Jongmyo jerye*), the *chuksa* (祝史, an official in charge of the ritual) puts the fur, blood, liver, and abdominal fat in trays. The livers are washed in *ulchangju* (鬱鬯酒, wine made of turmeric root), and everything is put into food vessels. The sacrifices are boiled and the fur and blood will be buried after completing the ritual.

[Singwan (晨祼)] On the ritual day, the *gungwiryeong* opens the doors of each chamber and tidies up the rooms; other officials bring in utensils used for food offerings, and another official inspects the setting. At 12:15 in the morning, all officiants participating in the actual ritual, wearing their ritual costume, and all assisting officials in court attire get ready by standing at their appointed positions. The *jiprye* proceeds with other officiants to a bowing place on the northern side of the *heonga* ensemble, where they bow four times, and return to their appointed positions. The *jeonak* leads the musicians and dancers to their appointed positions, and the officiants in charge of the second wine offering and others are also led to their respective positions. At 12:45 in the morning, the *myosa* (廟司, an officiant in charge of cleansing the shrine), *daechuk*, and *gungwiryeong* go up to the first chamber. At this time, the *chanin* opens the cabinet for the ancestral tablets. When the cabinet is open, the *daechuk* takes out the tablet of a deceased king and covers it with white ramie cloth, then places it on a table. Meanwhile, the *gungwiryeong* takes out the tablet of a deceased queen and covers it with blue ramie cloth, also placing it on the table. The other chambers follow the same procedure. When everyone returns to their original positions after finishing the process, an officiant washes and cleanses cups for wine and puts them in *junso* (尊所, a designated place for wine cups). When all the preparation is done, the king in *myeonbok* (冕服, king's formal ritual costume) enters through the front gate and stands at *panwi* facing west. When the *yeuisa* (禮儀使, an officiant in charge of announcing the procedure of the ritual) tells the king to start the ritual, the *hyeomnyullang* stands up holding up *hwi* (麾, a flag), an *akgong* (樂工, a musician) plays the *chuk*, and the *heonga* ensemble performs "Botaepyeongjiak" eight times while the dancers perform "Botaepyeongjimu." The king and officiants bow four times while the music is performed a ninth time as the procedure finishes. When the *hyeomnyullang* lays the flag down, a musician plays *eo* signaling the end of the music.

When the *jiprye* tells the participants to carry out Singwan–rye (晨祼禮, the procedure welcoming spirits at dawn), the king washes his hands, walks up the eastern stairs, and stands besides the *junso* facing west. At that time, the *deungga* ensemble plays "Botaepyeongjiak" and the *ilmu* is "Botaepyeongjimu." When the officiant charged with wine offering pours the *ulchangju*, another officiant receives it into a cup. The king stands in front of the ancestral tablet facing north, and then sits kneeling while the rest of the people also sit kneeling. When the *yeuisa* gives the order to burn incense three times, the other officiant places an incense burner on the table. The *jinpyechanjakgwan* (進幣瓚爵官, an officiant in charge of wine and gift offering) takes the wine cup and presents it to the king in a kneeling position. When the *yeuisa* asks the king to pour the wine onto the ground, the king does so.

• **Jeonpye (奠幣)** : When the *yeuisa* asks for the offering of a gift to the spirits, the *jinpyechanjakgwan* places the gift–a piece of white ramie cloth–and the king prostrates himself and then stands up. When the king emerges from the chamber and moves to other chambers, he repeats the same procedures of burning incense, pouring wine on the ground, and offering gifts as he did in the first chamber. When the king finishes the procedures, the *deungga* ensemble ends the music. With the *yeuisa* leading, the king walks down the eastern stairs and returns to his seat. When the *deungga* ensemble stops, each *chuksa* brings trays with the fur, blood, livers, and fat of the sacrifices, and puts them in front of the ancestral tablets. All the *chuksa* bring out livers, burn them in the brazier, and return to *junso*.

[Gwesik (饋食)] After the king finishes the procedure welcoming spirits at dawn, the *chanin*, leading *jeonsagwan* and other people in charge of food offerings, goes to the kitchen, and takes meat from the sacrificial cow, lamb, and pig from the cauldron, puts each of them in ceremonial utensils, leaving them in ceremonial storage for the food offerings.

• **Jinchan(進饌)** : When the *jiprye* announces the start of Jinchan (the procedure for food offerings), the *jeonsagwan* takes the sacrifices, in the order of cow, lamb, and pig, using the *bi* (匕, a ceremonial spoon), and puts them in *saenggap* (牲匣, ceremonial containers). The officiant makes one container of each sacrifice, for a total of three containers in each chamber. When the *cheonjogwan* (薦俎官, officiant in charge of presenting the sacrificial meats) holds up *jo* (俎, lit., "cutting board," a small ceremonial tray) for the first chamber, the *bongjogwan* (捧俎官, an officiant in charge of carrying the sacrifices) holding the *saenggap*, and *jeonsagwan*, holding other food offerings, walk in through the main gate, while the *heonga* ensemble plays "Punganjiak" (豊安之樂). The *chuksa* gives *mohyeolban* (毛血槃, the tray with the fur and blood of the sacrifices) to an officiant to take out. When the food offering reaches the central stairs, the *daechuk* leads the three officiants with the sacrificial and food offerings. The *cheonjogwan* goes to the first chamber, sits kneeling facing north, and presents the sacrificial meats in the order of cow, pig, and lamb. After finishing in the first chamber, he continues the same procedure in the subsequent chambers. The music ceases when the *cheonjogwan* finishes the procedure, and all officiants return to their positions. The *daechuk* takes mugwort and millet, rubs them with oil, burns them in the brazier, and returns to the *junso*. The officiants in charge of wine and gift offerings go up to the *junso* of the first chamber, and stand facing north.

• **Choheon (初獻)** : When the *jiprye* announces Choheon–rye (初獻禮, the procedure of the first wine offering), the king walks up the eastern stairs and stands at *junso*. At this time, the *deungga* ensemble plays

"Botaepyeongjiak" and the *ilmu* is "Botaepyeongjimu." The *jinpyechanjakgwan* pours the sweet wine and two other officiants receive it in two wine cups. When the king stands in front of the ancestral tablets facing north, and then sits kneeling, all other officiants also sit kneeling. When the *jinpyechanjakgwan* takes a wine cup from the officiant and presents it to the king in kneeling position, the king takes it and then gives the wine cup back to the *jinpyechanjakgwan*, who then takes the wine cup and presents it in front of the tablet of the deceased queen. When the *jinpyechanjakgwan* sits up after prostrating himself before the tablet, the music ends. The *daechuk* moves to the right side of the ancestral tablets facing east and recites the ceremonial prayer. When the recitation is done, the music begins. The king stands up after prostration, and all other participants do the same. The king passes through the door of the chamber into the hallway moving to other chambers in order to continue the wine offering procedure in each chamber. When the first wine offering is over, the music ends. The king walks down the eastern stairs and returns to his position. When the king enters his temporary ceremonial tent, the beaded hanging screen is taken down. The king comes back to *panwi* when "Jeongdaeeopjimu" is about to begin after "Botaepyeongjimu" is completed.

• **Aheon** (亞獻) : When the *jiprye* announces that Aheon–rye (亞獻禮, the procedure of the second wine offering) should proceed, the *aheongwan* (亞獻官, the officiant in charge of the second wine offering) washes his hands, ascends the eastern stairs, and stands on the *junso* of the first chamber facing west. The *heonga* ensemble plays "Jeongdaeeopjiak"; the *ilmu* is

"Jeongdaeeopjimu." When an officiant pours the wine, another officiant receives it in a wine cup. The *aheongwan* stands in front of the ancestral tablet facing north, and then sits kneeling. He takes the wine cup from an officiant in kneeling position, and then gives it back to the officiant having him present it to the tablets. The *aheongwan* presents the wine to the tablet of the deceased queen in the same manner. He lies prostrate, then stands up. Moving to other chambers, the *aheongwan* continues the second wine offering in the same manner. When the procedure is complete, the music stops. The *aheongwan* walks down and returns to his position.

• **Jongheon** (終獻) : The *jiprye* announces the start of Jongheon–rye (終獻禮, the procedure of the third wine offering). The *jongheongwan* (終獻官, the officiant in charge of the third wine offering) performs the procedure in the same manner as in the second wine offering. After completing the procedure, he returns to his position.

After finishing the third wine offering, the *chilsaheongwan* (七祀獻官, an officiant in charge of offerings to seven gods concerning the people's life) washes his hands, walks to the *junso*, and prepares himself for the offering procedures. When an officiant pours wine, another officiant takes it in a wine cup and gives it to the *chilsaheongwan*, who then presents the wine to the tablets of the gods in kneeling position. After prostrating himself, he sits kneeling. The *chuksa* reads the ceremonial prayer while kneeling and facing north. When the reading is done, the *chilsaheongwan* stands up. The *baehyanggongsin heonggwan* (配享功臣獻官, an officiant in charge of offerings to royal retainers whose tablets were enshrined in Jongmyo) offers the wine in the same manner as *chilsaheongwan*.

• **Eumboksujo** (飮福受胙) : When the *jongheongwan* goes back to his position, the *jeonpyechanjakgwan* and *cheonjogwan* walk up the eastern stairs and stand in the *eumbogwi* (飮福位, the place for partaking of sacrificial food and drink) facing north. The *daechuk* places some sacrificial meats located in front of the ancestral tablets onto *jo*. The king, who was in the temporary ceremonial tent emerges and stands in the *eumbogwi* facing west. The *jinpyechanjakgwan* takes the wine cup from the *daechuk*, and presents it to the king in a kneeling position. The king, also in a kneeling position, takes the wine cup and drinks it. After the *cheonjogwan* receives the *jo* with sacrificial meats from the *daechuk*, he presents it to the king. The king takes the *jo* and gives it to an officiant. The officiant with the *jo* walks down the eastern stairs and goes to the gate; he gives the *jo* to a court attendant of the food service bureau. The *jinpyechanjakgwan* and *cheonjogwan* go back to their positions. When the king stands straight after prostration, the rest of the people lie prostrate and then stand up. The king goes back to his position. After the king bows four times, the rest of the people also bow four times.

• **Cheolbyeondu** (徹籩豆) : When the *jiprye* announces Cheolbyeondu, an officiant slightly moves two ceremonial utensils–one *byeon* (籩, ceremonial utensil made of bamboo) and one *du* (豆, ceremonial utensil made of wood)–symbolically implying the removal of all offerings. The *deungga* ensemble plays "Onganjiak" (雍安之樂). The officiants charged with offerings to the seven gods and royal retainers also direct *cheolbyeondu*. When the procedure is completed, the music ends.

The *heonga* ensemble plays "Heunganjiak" (興安之樂). The king bows four times, and the rest of the officiants also bow four times. The musicians play the piece only one time and end. When the *yeuisa* announces that the royal ancestral ritual is ended, the king returns to the palace of the shrine, and leaves through the main gate. The king removes his formal ritual costume.

• **Mangye** (望瘞) : When the *jiprye* announces the Mangye (the procedure of observing burying *pyebaek* (幣帛, the offered gift)), the *aheongwan* stands facing north in the *mangyewi* (望瘞位, a place designated for observance). All *daechuk* take cooked millet and tie it up with a white string. They put the tied rice lumps, wooden slabs on which ceremonial prayers are written, and *pyebaek* into a basket, and walk down the western stairs to place the contents of the basket into a pit. When the *jiprye* gives the order to bury them, the court attendants bury them only up to half of the pit under the supervision of the *myosa*. The *aheongwan* and all the primary officiants leave the shrine. All officiants who had been in charge of supervising the ritual go to the place designated for bowing at the north side of the *heonga* ensemble, and bow four time before they leave the shrine. Musicians and dancers are leaving. The *daechuk*, with other officials, rearrange the ancestral tablets to their ordinary condition. All assisting officiants go to the place for bowing, and bow four times before they leave the shrine. The *chilsaheongwan* goes to the southern area of a pit in which wooden prayer boards for the seven gods will be buried outside the west gate, and stands facing north. An officiant buries the prayer boards and leaves. The *myosa* and other officiants put away all the food offered on the ceremonial tables. The *gungwiryeong* closes all the doors and leaves.

[Geogahwangung (車駕還宮)] When the king returns to the palace in the shrine, an officiant in charge of the ritual asks the king to lift the vigilance of the ritual. On 1 *gak* (一刻, at fifteen minutes after the hour), the drum signals the first command, and the royal guards get ready for the procession. When the drum signals the second command at three quarters of an hour, the large palanquin is set outside the main gate while the small palanquin is prepared facing south in front of the palace in the shrine. The royal guards get set for departure. When the drum signals the third command one hour after the first command, the crown prince comes out of the ceremonial tent and goes to the place designated for escorting the king. As preparations for the king's departure are completed, the king in his court attire riding on the small palanquin moves out to the main gate with the royal procession. As the small palanquin arrives at the outside of the main gate, the king changes to the large palanquin. The king's royal procession moves toward the king's palace as *gochwiak* (鼓吹樂, lit. "drumming and blowing" music) is played. When the royal procession arrives at the gate of Geunjeongjeon in Gyeongbok Palace, musicians stop playing *gochwiak*, and the king changes to a small palanquin in order to enter into the palace. When an *akgong* plays *chuk*, music begins.

When the king reaches the office building of the ceremonial ritual bureau, an *akgong* plays *eo* to stop the music, and the entourage escorts the king to the courtyard and withdraws.

[Chingha (稱賀)] As all the officiants gather in formation in the courtyard of Geunjeongjeon, the *chisagwan* (致詞官, an officiant in charge of delivering appreciation) congratulates them on their success in *Jongmyo jerye*.

Hitherto, the procedures of *Jongmyo jerye* have been examined based on the written records in *Gukjooryeui*. According to the document, the order of *Jongmyo jerye* is Jaegye, Jinseol, Geogachulgung, Seongsaenggi, Singwan, Jeonpye, Gwesik, Jinchan, Choheon, Aheon, Jongheon, Eumboksujo, Cheolbyeondu, Mangye, Geogahwangung, and Chingha. This differs somewhat from the current understanding of the order of *Jongmyo jerye*, which starts with Yeongsin and continues through Jeonpye, Jinchan, Choheon, Aheon, Jongheon, Eumbok, Cheolbyeondu, Songsin, and Mangryo. In terms of contents, the two orders are the same; however, the procedures of Yeongsin and Songsin were not written as entries in *Gukjooryeui*. In addition, at the time of *Gukjooryeui*, Mangye (observing burying the gifts and the prayers) was practiced instead of Mangnyo (observing burning the gifts and the prayers). Mangye was replaced with Mangnyo in 1757 (the thirty-third year of Yeongjo's reign).

Among the procedures of *Jongmyo jerye*, music and dance are performed in Yeongsin, Jeonpye, Jinchan, Choheon, Aheon, Jongheon,

Cheolbyeondu, and Songsin.

The procedures of *Jongmyo jerye* as seen in *Gukjooryeui* are still practiced today. *Jongmyo jerye* was designated as Important Intangible Cultural Heritage No. 56, and, before that, *Jongmyo jeryeak* was designated as Important Intangible Cultural Heritage No. 1, on December 7, 1964 by the Korean government. Both the ritual and its music have been designated as Masterpieces of the Oral and Intangible Heritage of Humanity by UNESCO on May 18, 2001. Also, the Jongmyo Shrine itself was designated Historic Site No. 125 by the Korean government as well as selected as World Cultural Heritage Site No. 738 on December 6, 1995. Jeongjeon (the main shrine) was designated National Treasure No. 227, and Yeongnyeongjeon (the sub–main shrine), Treasure No. 821. Jongmyo, the space in which the ritual music is performed, and *Jongmyo jerye*, the ritual in which the music becomes alive, have been preserved as precious cultural heritage. Jongmyo and the cultural heritage related to it are exceptional examples in which the edifice, the ritual, and the music have been wholly kept and transmitted. Currently, *Jongmyo jeryeak* is performed annually during the royal ancestral ritual held at Jongmyo on the first Sunday in May.

Today, the main shrine of Jongmyo contains only the ancestral tablets of nineteen kings–eighteen kings and one honorary king–out of the twenty–seven kings of the Joseon Dynasty; the rest are located in the sub–main shrine. The tablets for Yeonsan–gun (燕山君, r. 1494–1506) and Gwanghae–gun (光海君, r. 1609–1623), who were demoted to a lower rank, do not exist because Jongmyo symbolizes the authenticity of the dynasty.

The Origin and History of *Jongmyo jeryeak*

The Origin and History of *Jongmyo jeryeak*

1 . Historical Understanding of *Jongmyo jeryeak*

The history of *Jongmyo jeryeak* can be divided into three periods : The first is the era in which *daeseongaak* (大晟雅樂, a ritual music imported from the Song Dynasty in China) and *hyangak* were first used together as *Jongmyo jeryeak*. The second period extended until 1464 (the tenth year of King Sejo's reign). And the third period dates from after 1464, when *Botaepyeong* and *Jeongdaeeop*–which had originally been created by King Sejong as court banquet music–were chosen for use as *Jongmyo jeryeak*. The *Jongmyo jeryeak* of the first and second periods is different from the present–day music, which, by contrast, is directly related to the music from the third period.

However, although the music from the first and second periods is not directly related to current *Jongmyo jeryeak*, the establishment of the ritual, its instruments, and some melodies are partially related to the later ceremony, and so I begin this chapter by examining *Jongmyo jeryeak* from the Goryeo Dynasty. *Goryeosa* (高麗史, *History of Goryeo*) contains relatively detailed records regarding the *Jongmyo jeryeak* of the Goryeo period.

The *Jongmyo jeryeak* of the Goryeo Dynasty begins with the ceremonial entry of the king into the gate of the shrine. In addition, while the king made his way to the *gwansewi* (盥洗位, place for washing hands), and during the *gwanchang* (灌鬯, pouring wine on the ground), and *jinjo* (進俎walking up the stairs) procedures, "Jeonganjigok," "Sunanjigok," and "Punganjigok" were performed, respectively. Another characteristic of *Jongmyo jeryeak* in the Goryeo period is that the Eumbok (partaking of sacrificial food and drink) procedure was conducted immediately after Choheon, not after Jongheon as is done today. Except for these matters, though, the overall framework of the ritual in Goryeo times was similar to later practice. Regarding music, the imported Chinese ritual music and native Korean music were both used, with *aak* played during most procedures except Aheon and Songsin, in which native Korean music was used.

During the Joseon Dynasty, *Jongmyo jeryeak* underwent several alterations. At the time of the nation's founding, Joseon *Jongmyo jeryeak* followed the Goryeo tradition. According to records in the *Annals of King*

Taejong,[1] the king sent a diplomatic letter to the Ming Dynasty of China, asking "As the instruments used for Jongmyo and Sajik in this country are greatly damaged, allow us to buy the instruments." However, this request was not fulfilled because there were almost no instruments sold privately. Yet, in 1416 (the sixth year of King Taejong's reign), the Ming government sent envoys who delivered sixteen *pyeonjong*, sixteen *pyeongyeong*, four *geum* (琴, 7–stringed zither), two *seul* (瑟, 25–stringed zither) two *saeng*, and four *so*. Later the same year, these instruments were used for the first time at *Jongmyo jerye* held in autumn, in which King Taejong himself served as a priest.[2] As the account illustrates, during the early period of the Joseon Dynasty, Chinese–style *aak* was used for *Jongmyo jeryeak*, and the *ilmu*, "Yeolmunjimu" (烈文之舞) and "Somujimu" (昭武之舞) were performed as part of the ritual. Also, the tradition of playing native Korean music for Aheon and Songsin was maintained. However, the tradition of alternating between Chinese–style *aak* and native Korean music in *Jongmyo jeryeak* continued only until the early Joseon years, after which the practice changed to the sole use of *aak* in 1427 (the ninth year of King Sejong's reign).[3]

In 1430 (the twelfth year of King Sejong's reign), a group of scholar–officials, led by Pak Yeon, modified *Jongmyo jeryeak*, and made a separation

1) *Taejong sillok* (*The Annals of King Taejong*) Vol. 12, articles from the sixth year of King Taejong's reign, on 13 July (intercalary month).

2) *Taejong sillok* (*The Annals of King Taejong*) Vol. 12, articles from the sixth year of King Taejong's reign, on 9 October.

3) *Sejong sillok* (*The Annals of King Sejong*) Vol. 38, articles from the ninth year of King Sejong's reign, on 21, December.

between *yangyul* (陽律, lit., "yang pitch"; the odd–number notes of the twelve half–step scale) and *eumnyeo* (陰呂, lit., "yin pitch"; the even–number notes), applying the distinction to music played by the *deungga* and *heonga* ensembles. For instance, a piece in *hyeopjonggung* of *eumnyeo* was used in the *deungga* ensemble, while a piece in *muyeokgung* of *yangyul* was played by the *heonga* ensemble. This musical change was made based on the records in *Seokjeonakbo* (釋奠樂譜, *Confucius Shrine Ritual Notation*), written by Im U(林宇). In the previous tradition of *Jongmyo jeryeak* from the Goryeo Dynasty, the *deungga* and *heonga* ensembles would both use pieces in *muyeokgung*, without making a distinction between *yangyul* and *eumnyeo*.

Different musical pieces were performed in each chamber during the Choheon–rye. When Choheon was conducted in the chamber for Mokjo (穆祖, ?–1274, great–great–grandfather of King Taejo), "Sunnyeongjigok" (純寧之曲) was performed; while in the chamber for Ikjo (翼祖, dates of birth and death unknown, great–grandfather), "Sonyeongjigok" (紹寧之曲) was played; in the chamber for Dojo (度祖, ?–1342, grandfather), "Jeongmyeongjigok" (貞明之曲); in the chamber for Hwanjo (桓祖, 1315–1361, father), "Wimyeongjigok" (威明之曲); and for King Taejo himself, "Somyeongjigok" (紹寧之曲) was played. The *Jongmyo jeryeak* of King Sejong's time was maintained until 1463 (King Sejo's ninth year), when *Botaepyeong* and *Jeongdaeeop* replaced the previous music.

2. *Botaepyeong* and *Jeongdaeeop* : The Prototype of *Jongmyo jeryeak*

Originally, *Botaepyeong* and *Jeongdaeeop* were created as court banquet music. King Sejong himself, an expert in music, composed the pieces. The following is from the *Annals of King Sejong* in 1449 :

> The king told Seungjeongwon (the secretary's office of the king) that "Although the newly-composed music cannot replace *aak*, it will not be abolished because the music describes the achievements of ancestors and the past kings. After Uijeongbu (the highest office of government) and Gwanseupdogam (a governmental office in charge of music) examine the music and report to me whether they are pro or con toward the music, I will certainly calculate the gains and losses." The king had a depth of understanding in music. The rhythm of the newly-composed music was decided by the king as he set syllables by stamping a stick onto the ground one evening . . . First, the king ordered Pak Yeon to tune the pitch of the instruments. When Pak Yeon demonstrated the tune of *okgyeong* (玉磬, a set of stone chimes), the king listened to it and said "the pitch of the *ichik* (夷則, the ninth note of the twelve half-step scale) stone chime is slightly high, so if you grind the stone a little the pitch will be balanced." When Pak Yeon took the stone chime and examined it, the king's words turned out to be true : there were some parts which the maker of the instrument forgot to round off evenly.[4)]

4) *Sejong sillok* (*The Annals of King Sejong*) Vol. 126, articles from the thirty–first year of King Sejong's reign, on 11 December.

The newly–composed pieces by King Sejong were *Botaepyeong*, *Jeongdaeeop*, *Balsang*, and *Bongnaeui*. It is recorded that these are the music that King Sejong himself composed, setting their rhythms by striking a stick on the ground one evening. One might question whether the record is true or not, yet considering the composition method in use at the time of King Sejong, it is quite likely. At that time, it was common that new musical pieces were created through a method called *suribujak* (述而不作) which, unlike the modern way of composition, applied texts to pre–existing melodies by changing rhythms to fit the new text. Therefore, the record saying that the new pieces were composed "on one evening" should be understood in terms of the composing method of the time.

Botaepyeong and *Jeongdaeeop*, set by King Sejong, were created based on *hyangak* and *gochwiak*. *Botaepyeong* consists of eleven pieces while *Jeongdaeeop* includes fifteen pieces.

① The eleven pieces of *Botaepyeong* :

"Huimun" (熙文), "Gyeu" (啓宇), "Uiin" (依仁), "Hyeonggwang" (亨光), "Boye" (保乂), "Yunghwa" (隆化), "Seunggang" (承康), "Changhwi" (昌徽), "Jeongmyeong" (貞明), "Daedong" (大同), "Yeokseong" (繹成)

② The fifteen pieces of *Jeongdaeeop* :

"Somu" (昭武), "Dokgyeong" (篤慶), "Seonwi" (宣威), "Takryeong" (濯靈), "Hyeokjeong" (赫整), "Sinjeong" (神定), "Gaean" (凱安), "Jideok" (至德), "Hyumyeong" (休命), "Suneung" (順應), "Jeongse" (靖世), "Hwatae" (和泰),

"Jinyo" (震耀), "Sukje" (肅制), "Yeonggwan" (永觀)

These pieces were created from *gochwiak*, which included various tunes at that time, as well as *hyangak* from the Goryeo Dynasty, such as "Pungipsong (風入松)," "Manjeonchun (滿殿春)," "Seogyeong byeolgok (西京別曲)," and "Cheongsan byeolgok (青山別曲)." When adopting these pieces as music for the ancestral ritual, some were partially selected while some others were dropped entirely; eventually, eleven pieces of *Botaepyeong* and eleven pieces from *Jeongdaeeop* were settled on.

3. Adoption of *Botaepyeong* and *Jeongdaeeop* as *Jongmyo jeryeak*

In 1464, prototypes of the current *Botaepyeong* and *Jeongdaeeop* were adopted as *Jongmyo jeryeak*. King Sejo recognized the musical value of *Botaepyeong* and *Jeongdaeeop* even before he became king. When he was a prince, King Sejo commended dozens of the court ladies to learn the music, contributing to preservation of the performing tradition in the palace.[5)] Also, since he felt regret that the newly-composed pieces by King Sejong had not been properly used, he searched for a way to transmit them.

5) *Sejong sillok* (*The Annals of King Sejong*) Vol. 126, articles from the thirty-first year of King Sejong's reign, on 11 December.

> [The King] sent a letter to Akhakdogam (樂學都監, a governmental office for music study) stating "Establishing *ye* (禮, proper decorum) and creating *ak*(樂, music) could be done only by saints. Therefore, there had been no one who could amend and renew them, even after myriad years, because it is difficult to have a saint in this world. The collapse of *ye* and unbalancing of *ak* are caused because of this. King Sejong established many kinds of music and dance with the wisdom granted by the heaven, yet these had not been properly practiced. Although today, literary refinement and training in the martial arts leave no room for other things, wouldn't it be regrettable that it will fall into disuse if we do not carry it out? Also, as musicians do not belong to the military, and they should learn music all the time at the music bureau, from now on learn the new music of *Jeongdaeeop*, *Botaepyeong*, *Balsang*, and *Bongnaeui*, and discard all the old music. Make a prompt report on the numbers of musicians and instruments, and the repertoires of pieces they are practicing after discussion."[6)]

This command was issued in 1460, only six years after King Sejo's enthronement. King Sejo wanted to abandon the old music, replacing it with the music newly–composed by King Sejong. After this order, in 1463, King Sejo called on the *Akhakjejo* (樂學提調, a high–ranking position in the music bureau) Yang Seong–ji and Seong Im, ordering them to have *gongin* (工人, a generic term for court musicians) perform *Botaepyeong* and *Jeongdaeeop*, and to have *aksaeng* (樂生, court musicians in charge of *aak*) dance. Furthermore, the

6) *Sejo sillok* (*The Annals of King Sejo*) Vol. 20, articles from the sixth year of King Sejo's reign, on 22 April.

king ordered the shortening of the length of *Botaepyeong* and *Jeongdaeeop* to fit the length of the ancestral ritual.

> The king ordered simplifying *Botaepyeong* and *Jeongdaeeop* composed by King Sejong because, as they have too many phrases in their texts, it was not possible to perform all the pieces during the ritual. The king also decided the music and dance in the ritual for the worship of heaven. In fact, there were music and dance already; however, because the Jinchan, Cheolbyeondu, and Songsin procedures did not have music, Choe Hang and others asked the king, and the king commanded Choe Hang to compose lyrics.[7)]

As is documented here, Choe Hang revised the texts of the music by shortening the lengthy lyrics, and composed new texts for music in the Jinchan, Cheolbyeondu, and Songsin procedures, so as to make *Botaepyeong* and *Jeongdaeeop* suitable as ancestral ritual music. This renewed music was performed for the first time as *Jongmyo jeryeak* in the spring ancestral ritual held in lunar January of 1464, inaugurating the history of the current *Jongmyo jeryeak*. In *Sejo sillok*, the music and dance used at the time is documented.[8)]

> Yeongsin : "Botaepyeongjiak" and "Botaepyeongjimu" in *heonga.*
>
> Jeonpye : "Botaepyeongjiak" and "Botaepyeongjimu" in *deungga.*

---

7) *Sejo sillok* (*The Annals of King Sejo*) Vol. 31, articles from the ninth year of King Sejo's reign, on 15 November.

8) *Sejo sillok* (*The Annals of King Sejo*) Vol. 48, Akbo (Music)

Jinchan : "Punganjiak" in *heonga*.

Choheon : "Botaepyeongjiak" and "Botaepyeongjimu" in *deungga*.

Aheon : "Jeongdaeeopjiak" and "Jeongdaeeopjimu" in *heonga*.

Jongheon : "Jeongdaeeopjiak" and "Jeongdaeeopjimu" in *heonga*.

Cheolbyeondu : "Onganjiak" in *deungga*.

Songsin : "Heunganjiak" in *heonga*.

The *Akbo* section of *Sejo sillok* indicates the orchestrations of the *deungga* and *heonga* ensembles by configuration. The *deungga* ensemble consists of a *teukjong*, a *teukgyeong*, a *pyeongjong*, a *pyeongyeong*, a *bak* (clapper), a *chuk*, an eo, a *daejaeng*, an *ajaeng*, six singers, a *hyeongeum* (or *geomungo*), a *banghyang*, a *gayageum*, a *hwa*, a *saeng*, two *dangbipa*, a *wolgeum*, two *janggu*, a *jeolgo*, a *hun*, a *ji*, two *dangjeok*, two *daegeum*, a *tungso*, two *pilryul* (or *piri*), and a *haegeum*. The *heonga* ensemble contains a *bak*, four sets of *pyeongjong*, two sets of *pyeongyeong*, eight singers, a *hyangbipa*, four *dangbipa*, a *hyeongeum*, two sets of *banghyang*, a *gayageum*, a *wolgeum*, two *taepyeongso*, six *pilryul*, six *janggo*, a *hwa*, two *u*, a *saeng*, two *tungso*, two *dangjeok*, four *daegeum*, two *junggeum*, two *sogeum*, and a *gyobanggo*, besides two sets of *nogo* and two sets of *nodo* that are indispensable in the rites for the human spirit. These orchestrations include all instruments from *aak*, *hyangak*, and *dangak*, as well as the *pareum* system, demonstrating the fulfillment of all the requisite characteristics for *Jongmyo jeryeak* appearing on stage for the first time.

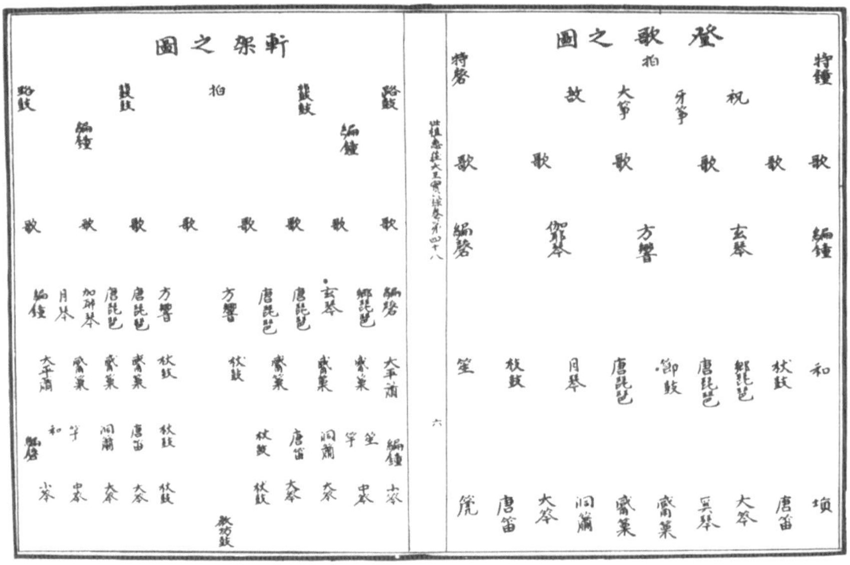

Figure13. Arrangement of *deungga* (right) and *heonga* (left) ensembles in *Sejo sillok*

In addition, the configurations for *ilmu*, including both the *munmu* of *Botaepyeong* and *mumu* of *Jeongdaeeop*, appear in the *Akbo* section of *Sejo sillok*. It is particularly notable that, in the *Jeongdaeeop mumu*, the usage of the flags of the honor guard–*hwangnyonggi* (黃龍旗, the flag of yellow dragon), *baekhogi* (白虎旗, the flag of white tiger), *jujakgi* (朱雀旗, the flag of red phoenix), and *hyeonmugi* (玄武旗, the flag of *hyeonmu*[9])–and other instruments used by the honor guard in the configuration manifest the meaning of the dance as it praises military achievements.

The order and content of the music and dance that were performed

9) The *hyeonmu* is a mystical animal that combines the shapes of a turtle and a snake.

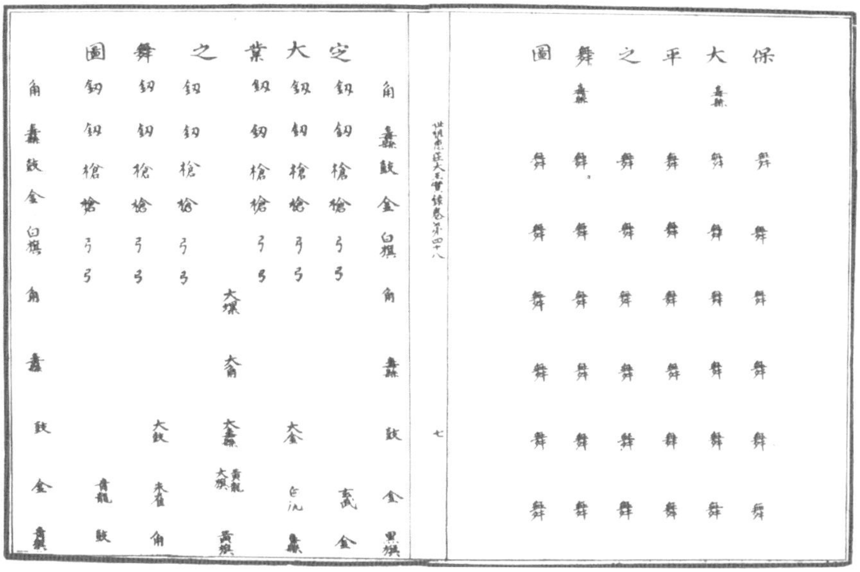

Figure 14. Arrangement of *munmu* (right) and *mumu* (left) in *Sejo sillok*

in *Jongmyo jerye* in the spring of 1464 are identical to those in the current *Jongmyo jerye*. To understand the *Jongmyo jerye* of 1464 in the overall context of the ritual structure, it is indispensable to reference the written documents regarding the ritual in *Sejo sillok*. The record of January 14, 1464 (the tenth year of Sejo's reign) in *Sejo sillok* begins as follows : "The king himself served at *Jongmyo jerye*, and the newly–created music of *Jeongdaeeop* and *Botaepyeong* were performed, and the ritual is as follows."[10)]

It was a historical moment. King Sejo learned the music and dance that his father King Sejong created when he was a prince, and worried that

10) *Sejo sillok* (*The Annals of King Sejo*) Vol. 32, articles from the tenth year of King Sejo's reign, on 14 January.

it might be disused. Eventually, King Sejo ensured that the music and dance would be continually performed and listened to in Jongmyo. The following are details on *Jongmyo jerye* from the time of King Sejo.

[Singwan] On the day of *Jongmyo jerye*, the *gungwiryeong* opens the door of each chamber and tidies up the rooms. *Jongmyoryeong* (宗廟令, an official in charge of Jongmyo shrine) and *jeonsagwan* bring in ceremonial utensils, and the *gamchal* examines the setting. At 12:15 in the morning, all *hyanggwan* (享官, officiants serving as priests) and *baejegwan* (陪祭官, officials participating in the ritual as general officiants, not priests) put on their costumes and go to their positions. Led by the *aakryeong* (雅樂令, the head of musicians), all *gongin*, and *munmu* and *mumu* dancers enter and take their positions. The royal family, who assists in the ritual, all civil and military functionaries, *aheongwan*, and *hyanggwan* take their positions. As everyone enters, they bow four times. After that, when the preparation for the ritual is completed, the *daechuk*, *jongmyoryeong*, and *gungwiryeong* enter into Hwanjosil (桓祖室, the chamber of the father of King Taejo), and open the cabinet of the ancestral tablet. After opening the cabinet, the *daechuk* and *gungwiryeong* take out the tablet and set it on its designated place on the ceremonial table. The same procedure takes place in the chambers of King Taejo and others born after King Taejo. All the ceremonial wine cups are washed. When all preparations are completed, the king in his formal ritual costume enters through the main gate and stands at *panwi* facing west. The *heonga* ensemble performs "Botaepyeongjiak" and the *ilmu* is "Botaepyeongjimu." The king and all others bow four times. *Jinpyechanjakgwan* and *jeonpyechanjakgwan* go to the place for washing, wash their hands, and proceed to *junso* of Hwanjosil facing north.

• **Jeonpye** : The king goes to the place for washing, washes his hands, and walks up the east stairs. He goes to *junso* of Hwanjosil, and stands there facing west. The *deungga* ensemble plays "Botaepyeongjiak" with *ilmu* "Botaepyeongjimu." When the *jinpyechanjakgwan* scoops up *ulchangju*, the other officiant receives it in a ceremonial wine cup. When the king stands in front of the tablet facing north, the *yeuisa* tells him to burn incense three times. The king does so. Then, the *yeuisa* asks him to pour the wine onto the ground, and the king holds the wine cup and pours the wine so the spirit would comes down. The king holds *pyebaek*, and presents it on the ceremonial table in kneeling position. The king repeats the same procedures of burning incense, pouring wine onto the ground, and presenting *pyebaek* in Taejosil (太祖室, the chamber for King Taejo), Gongjeongwangsil (恭靖王室, the chamber for King Jeongjong), Taejongsil (太宗室, the chamber for King Taejong), Sejongsil (世宗室, the chamber for King Sejong), and Munjongsil (文宗室, the chamber for King Munjong). When the king finishes, the music ceases. The king walks down the east stairs and goes back to his place. When the *deungga* ensemble ends the music, all *chuksa* present *mohyeolban* and fat from the sacrifices.

[Gwesik] When the king finishes the procedures to call the spirits, the *jeonsagwan* and other officiants in charge of food offering go to the kitchen led by a *chanin*, take the cow, lamb, and pig meats, each in ceremonial pots, and everything is put into the ceremonial food vessel.

• **Jinchan** : When the *jiprye* calls out "Jinchan," the *jeonsagwan scoops* the sacrificial meats, using a ceremonial spoon, in the order of cow, lamb, and pig, into *saenggap*, making one container for each meat for each chamber. The *cheonjogwan*, holding up the *jo* for Hwanjosil, and the *bongjogwan*, holding up *saenggap*, enter the main gate, and when the *jo* enters the gate, the *heonga* ensemble plays "Punganjiak." All the *chuksa* give *mohyeolban* to an officiant to go out. When the food offering reaches the central stairs, all *daechuk* lead the officiants holding the food offering. The *cheonjogwan* goes to the tablet of Hwanjosil, and presents the sacrificial meats in the order of cow, lamb, and pig. After that, the *cheonjogwan* continues to move to other chambers, in the order of Taejosil, Gongjeongwangsil, Taejongsil, Sejongsil, and Munjongsil, repeating the procedure in the same manner. When the procedure is done, the music ends, and all officiants go back to their positions. All *daechuk* take mugwort and millet, rub them with oil, burn them over a charcoal fire in a brazier, and go back to *junso*.

• **Choheon** : When the *jiprye* announces Choheon–rye, the king walks up the eastern stairs and stands at *junso* of Hwanjosil. The *deungga* ensemble plays "Botaepyeongjiak" and the *ilmu* is "Botaepyeongjimu." The *jinpyechanjakgwan* pours the sweet wine and two other officiants receive it in wine cups. When the king stands in front of the ancestral tablets facing north, and then sits kneeling, all other officiants also sit kneeling. The *jinpyechanjakgwan* takes a wine cup from the officiant and presents it to the king. The king gives the wine cup back to the *jinpyechanjakgwan* so as to present it to the tablet. After that, the first wine offering is presented to the deceased queen in the same manner. When the procedure is done, the music ceases. The *daechuk* recites the ceremonial prayer, and when the recitation is done, the music begins. The king stands up after prostration, and all other participants do the same. When the king passes out the door of the chamber, the music ends. The king moves on to other chambers, and repeats Choheon–rye in the same manner. When the procedure is over, the music ends. The king walks down the eastern stairs and goes back to his position. When the king enters into his temporal ceremonial tent, the dancers for "Botaepyeongjimu" withdraw, and the dancers for "Jeongdaeeopjimu" come out.

• **Aheon** : When the *jiprye* announces the start of Aheon–rye, the *bujitongrye* (副知通禮, an officiant assigned to assist the crown prince) leads *aheongwan*. If the crown prince does not serve in the Aheon procedure, the *alja* (謁者, an officiant in charge of leading the priests in the ritual) guides *aheongwan*. The *aheongwan* goes to the place for washing, washes his hands, and walks up the eastern stairs standing in front of Hwanjosil facing west. The *heonga* ensemble plays "Jeongdaeeopjiak" with *ilmu* "Jeongdaeeopjimu." When an officiant pours the wine, another officiant takes it in a wine cup. The *aheongwan* stands in front of the ancestral tablet facing north, and then sits kneeling. He takes the wine cup from an officiant, and then gives it back to the officiant, having him present it to the tablet. The *aheongwan* presents the wine to the tablet of the deceased queen in the same manner. After that, the Aheon procedure continues in other chambers in the same way. When the procedure is done, the music ceases.

• **Jongheon** : The *jiprye* announces Jongheon–rye. The *jongheongwan* performs the procedure, following the same steps as with the procedure for the second wine offering. After finishing the third wine offering procedure, the *chilsaheongwan* goes to the washing place, washes his hands, and serves the wine offering. When *chilsaheongwan* is positioned in front of the tablet, and sits kneeling facing west, an officiant gives him the wine cup, and the *chilsaheongwan* presents it to the tablet. When the *daechuk* finishes reading the written prayer, the *chilsaheongwan* stands up after prostrating himself, and goes back to his position. The *baehyanggongsin heonggwan* offers the wine in the same manner, and goes back to his position.

• **Eumboksujo** : When the *jongheongwan* goes back to his position, the *jeonpyechanjakgwan* and *cheonjogwan* walk up the eastern stairs and go to *eumbogwi*. The *daechuk* goes to the *junso* of Hwanjosil, scoops out some wine into the ceremonial cup, and takes out some sacrificial meats onto the *jo*. The king comes out of the temporal ceremonial tent, goes to *eumbogwi*, and sits kneeling facing west. The king takes the wine cup and drinks it. When the *yeuisa* asks the king to take the *jo* with sacrificial meats, the king takes it and gives back to an official. The officiant takes the *jo*, walks down the eastern stairs, goes to the gate, and gives it to a court attendant of the food service bureau. The *jinpyechanjakgwan* and *cheonjogwan* go back to their positions. When the king stands straight after prostrating himself, the rest of the people lie prostrate and then stand up. After the king returns to his position and bows four times, the rest of the people also bow four times.

• **Cheolbyeondu** : When the *jiprye* calls for Cheolbyeondu, an officiant slightly moves the vessels (one *byeon* and one *du*). The *deungga* ensemble plays "Onganjiak" (雍安之樂). The officiants charged with offerings to the seven gods and royal retainers also conduct Cheolbyeondu. When the procedure is completed, the music ends.

• **Songsin** : When the *jiprye* announces Songsin–rye (送信禮, the procedure for sending off spirits), the heonga ensemble plays "Heunganjiak" (興安之樂). When the music ends, the *yeuisa* reports to the king that the ritual is ended, and the king goes back to the palace of the shrine, where he takes off the formal ritual costume.

• **Mangye** : When the *jiprye* announces *mangye*, the *aheongwan* goes to *mangyewi* facing north. All *daechuk* bring lumps of cooked millet and tie each of them up with a white string. They put the tied rice lumps, wooden prayer holder, and *pyebaek* into a basket, and walk down the western stairs to put the contents of the basket into a pit. When the *jiprye* orders them to be buried, the court attendants bury them only halfway, under the supervision of the *jongmyoryeong*. The *aheongwan* and *hyanggwan* leave. The royal family and all civil and military functionaries leave. All officiants who had been in charge of supervising the ritual go to the place designated for bowing at the north side of the *heonga* ensemble, and bow four time before they leave. Led by the *aakryeong*, all musicians and dancers leave. *Jongmyoryeong*, *daechuk*, and *gungwiryeong* bring in the ancestral tablets. *Jeonsagwan* and *jongmyoryeong*, with their assisting officiants, remove the food offerings. The *gungwiryeong* closes the chamber doors, and leaves. The royal procession returns to the king's palace.

The steps detailed above reflect the scenario of the *Jongmyo jerye* ritual for which the newly–adopted *Jongmyo jeryeak* was played for the first time, performed along with its accompanying dance in lunar January of 1464. Scholar–official Kim Pil held overall responsibility for conducting the ritual. After its completion, King Sejo called in Pak Won–hyeong and No Sa–sin, high–ranking scholar–officials who served as *yeuisa* for the ritual, and bestowed a cup of wine on them. The king said "The new musical pieces just performed in the rite matched up well with the large–scale ritual so that there were no parts in conflict. I am well pleased to fulfill the will of King Sejong." Responding to this, Pak Won–hyeong answered, "If it had not been brought to success by Your Majesty, the will of King Sejong would have not been achieved."

It seems that because King Sejo had a sense of perfect pitch, he had a special affection for the music created by King Sejong, who also had outstanding musicality. Eventually, King Sejo made *Botaepyeong* and *Jeongdaeeop*–which he felt were great–the music for *Jongmyo jerye*, and he verified the sufficiency of the music to be used for the large–scale ritual by employing it in the actual rite. King Sejo's idea to use court banquet music as ancestral ritual music was a change of thinking that began the great history of *Jongmyo jeryeak*, which has continued its tradition for over 545 years. The procedure of *Jongmyo jerye* performed in the spring of 1464, in which the newly–adopted music was used, is almost identical to that of King Seongjong's time. In other words, from the tenth year of King Sejo's reign, *Jongmyo jeryeak* was transmitted without change until King Seongjong's era.

After King Sejo, *Jongmyo jeryeak* went through changes several times. In particular, after Byeongjahoran, *Jongmyo jeryeak* was not performed for about ten years; it was restored during the time of Gwanghae-gun. After the war, *Jongmyo jeryeak* was performed without all the necessary instruments. Because of this, the ensembles were downsized compared to those from the time of King Sejo or King Seongjong. In 1626 (the fourth year of King Injo's (仁祖, r. 1623–1649) reign), in *Botaepyeong*, "Junggwang" (重光) was added after "Jeongmyeong" to be used in the chamber of King Seonjo (宣祖, r. 1567–1608). Because King Seonjo was considered to be a king who enhanced national prestige and accomplished national restoration as he experienced the Imjinwaeran, it was considered proper to have a separate piece for him. In addition, because the piece used in the Choheon–rye was short, musicians performed another piece, and a new piece was composed to be inserted between "Jeongmyeong" and "Daeyu."

Second–vice premier Sin Heum suggested that each chamber should have its own *akjang*. At that time, "Huimun," "Gimyeong," "Gwiin," "Hyeongga," and "Jimnyeong" were performed for the four great ancestors, Mokjo, Ikjo, Dojo, and Hwanjo; "Yunghwa," was performed for King Taejong; "Daeyu," and "Yeokseong" were in common use for all chambers; "Dokgyeong" and "Takjeong" were for Mokjo and Hwanjo; "Seonwi," "Sinjeong," "Bunung," "Suneung," and "Chongyu" were for King Taejo; "Jeongse" was for King Taejong; "Hyeokjeong" was for King Sejong; and "Somu" and "Yeonggwan" were in common use. Sin Heum asserted that from a commonsense point of view, each chamber should have its own *akjang*, and the *akjang* used for the four great ancestors should not be performed in Jongmyo. Although he questioned why the tradition had not been corrected for hundreds of years, he answered himself that it might be because of keeping the traditional idea that "the ancestral ritual music has to follow the music for the person of the highest rank." However, he proposed to have Confucian scholars examine whether each chamber should have its own *akjang*, or if the emphasis of the music should follow the music of the highest–ranking people, by studying historical examples.[11] Like this example, there are many discussions regarding *akjang* in relation to *Jongmyo jeryeak* as it comes into the seventeenth century. This argument continued as the number of chambers in Jongmyo Shrine increased as kings passed away.

11) *Injo sillok* (*The Annals of King Injo*) Vol. 13, articles from the 4th year of King Injo's reign, on 25 June (intercalary month).

In the seventeenth century, the texts of the *akjang* performed for each chamber did not match the achievements of the king whose tablet was enshrined therein. Therefore, scholar–officials such as Hwang Jeong–uk, O Yun–gyeom, and Song Jun–gil proposed creating *akjang* that corresponded with the achievements of each enshrined king. However, scholar–officials such as Yi Jeong–gu, Nam Gu–man, and Yi Yeo suggested creating new *akjang* only for kings with meritorious deeds, since they understood the tradition of *akjang* as "because the ritual music follows the person of the highest rank, only King Taejo's and King Taejong's achievements had been praised, and separate texts were composed for common use with the rest of the chambers."

The arguments continued to the time of King Yeongjo, until eventually "Yonggwang" and "Jeongmyeong" became the single piece, "Yonggwang–Jeongmyeong," and the ninth piece was performed in all twelve chambers (at the time of King Yeongjo, there were twelve chambers). This tradition has continued until today.[12)]

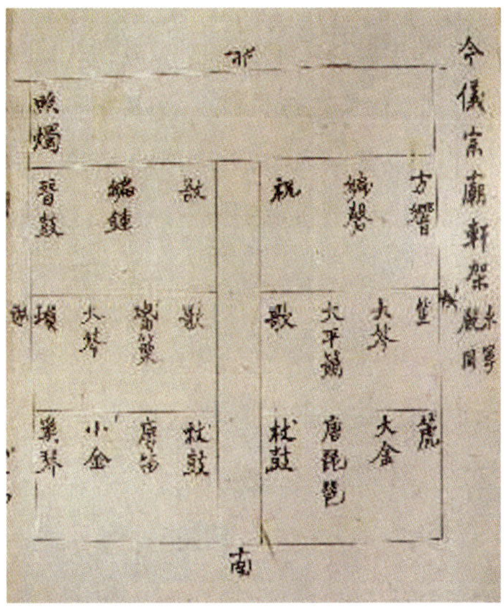

Figure 15. Arrangement of the *heonga* ensemble in *Chungwantonggo*

12) Song Ji-won, "Akwongosareul tonghae bon 17 segi jongmyoakjang nonwi" *Munheongwa haeseok* Vol. 15, 2001, Munheongwa haeseoksa.

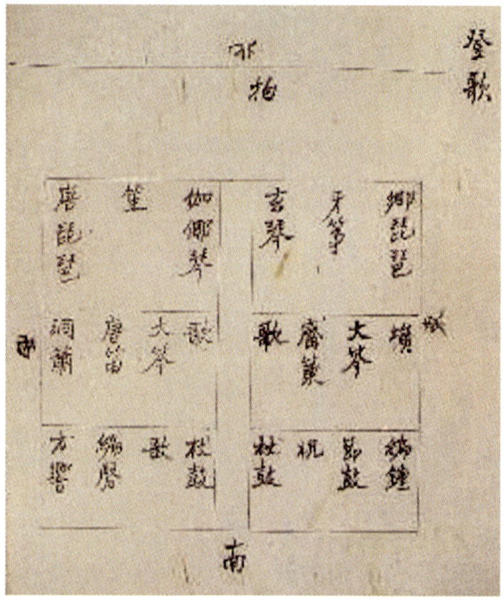

Figure 16. Arrangement of the *deungga* ensemble in *Chungwantonggo*

The orchestration of *Jongmyo jeryeak* was reduced in the latter part of the Joseon Dynasty. Although there were no substantial changes, several changes of detail were made in the time of King Jeongjo when the Jongmyo Shrine consisted of fourteen chambers in Jeongjeon and twelve chambers in Yeongnyeongjeon. In *Gukjooryeui*, the orchestration of *Jongmyo jeryeak* includes thirty-six musicians in the *deungga* ensemble and seventy musicians in the *heonga* ensemble, for a total of 106 musicians. However, in the time of King Jeongjo, the orchestration was decreased to twenty–three *deungga* musicians with twenty instruments, and twenty–two *heonga* musicians with nineteen instruments, a total of forty–five musicians.

The configuration of the *deungga* ensemble from the time of King Jeongjo is in four rows, running west to east. A *bak* is located in the center of the first, northernmost row. In the second row, centered on the *eodo* (御道, the king's way that is located in the middle of the second, third, and fourth rows), a *hyeongeum*, an *ajaeng*, and a *hyangbipa* are set in order, running from the center toward the edge on the east side of the *eodo*, while a *gayageum*, a *saeng*, and a *dangbipa* are set in the same manner on the west side. In the third row, a singer, a *pilryul*, a *daegeum*, and a *hun* are set from the center toward the edge on the east side of the *eodo*, while on west side, a singer, a *daegeum*, a *dangjeok*, and a *tungso* are set in the fashion, progressing toward the west. On the east side of the fourth row, a *janggo*, a *chuk*, a *jeolgo*, and a *pyeonjong* are positioned, in order from the center to the east, and on the west side, a *janggo*, an *eo*, a *pyeongyeong*, and a *banghyang* are set, in order to the west. This demonstrates that the orchestration comprises all *hyangak*, *dangak*, and *aak* instruments. Furthermore, it is true that the number of instruments is reduced, compared to the previous era; however, it could be said that the orchestration is well–maintained in terms of furnishing all *pareum* materials.

When the orchestration of the *deungga* ensemble from the time of King Jeongjo is compared to that in the era of King Sukjong (肅宗, r. 1674–1720), based on *Jongmyouigwe* (宗廟儀軌, *Code of Courtesy for Jongmyo jerye*), there are no significant differences. Only several instruments and musicians were added : a *saeng*, a *hun*, and an *eo* were included; a *sogeum*, a *bak*, and a *nodo* were not included in the *heonga* ensemble; and the number of *piri* was reduced from two to one.

On the one hand, the reason that instruments were added was to complete the orchestration in terms of the rule requiring inclusion of all *pareum* instruments. On the other hand, it was because it became possible to purchase instruments that were not manufactured in Joseon, and musicians were able to learn playing techniques. For instance, in the case of *saenghwang*, it was not possible to produce the right pitches with it in 1765 (the forty–first year of King Yeongjo's reign). *Jeonak* Jang Cheon–ju was told to purchase the *saeng* and learn its playing technique when he was sent to China as a member of a delegation, so that the *saeng* became a usable instrument.

At the time of King Jeongjo, a significant change took place regarding the location where *ilmu* was performed. Compared to the current Jongmyo Shrine, the shrine in the early period of the Joseon Dynasty had limited space. Because of this, the *ilmu* had to be positioned diagonally in the west part of the courtyard during the ritual. However, the location of the *ilmu* was continually pointed out as a mistake. Although this problem was actively discussed in the second half of the Joseon Dynasty, especially during the time of King Sukjong, no solution was arrived at. During the time of King Jeongjo, with an appeal by military–official Yu Ui-yang, the location of *ilmu* was changed to the center of the courtyard.

In 1787 (the eleventh year of King Jeongjo's reign), Yu Ui–yang pointed out that the *ilmu* was not in line with the *deungga* and *heonga* ensembles because of the location of the dancers, and that this was not proper decorum. He noted that, because Jongmyo Shrine had been expanded to fourteen chambers, and the east side as well as the west side of the courtyard was enlarged, there was no reason to keep the tradition that did not correspond to proper decorum. Eventually, his appeal was accepted. Later, the location of the *yugilmu*–thirty–six dancers in six lines–moved in–line with the ensembles, by putting three lines on the east side of *jeongno* (正路, the main road) and another three lines on the west side of it. In the time of King Jeongjo, this system was kept and practiced. However, in the current *Jongmyo jerye*, the *ilmu* is located on the west side of *jeongno*, because sometime after King Jeongjo, the *ilmu* location was changed again.

The current *Jongmyo jeryeak* has changed significantly since the nineteenth century, especially during the Japanese occupation. At that time, all the string instruments–*geomungo*, *gayageum*, and *hyangbipa*–were excluded, and the rhythmic structure was changed. In the case of *akjang*, the parts removed under the Japanese colonial government were recovered; however, the orchestration and rhythmic structure have not been restored to their original forms even today.

Figure 17. *Heonga* ensemble

Musical Accompaniment in the Royal Ancestral Ritual

Musical Accompaniment in the Royal Ancestral Ritual

From ancient times, instrumental performance, singing, and dancing have been considered indispensable to sacrificial rites,[1)] and that tradition has been maintained in *Jongmyo jeryeak*. This chapter explores the ensembles and their instrumentation, the procedure of the ritual and its music, and the music scores and their musical characteristics.

1. Ensembles and Instrumentation

Although *Jongmyo jeryeak* is indigenous Korean music, its

1) Min-su Yi, *Commentary on Yegi* (Seoul : Hyewon chulpansa, 1995), 549.

instrumentation follows the *aak* system. In *aak*, it is normal to have *deungga* and *heonga* ensembles : the *deungga* ensemble primarily consists of singing and string instruments, while the *heonga* ensemble is formed with wind and percussion instruments. In addition, the *heonga* ensemble uses four different instrumentations according to the status of the subject of the rite : *gunghyeon* for an emperor, *heonhyeon* for a feudal lord, *panhyeon* for a noble lord, and *teukhyeon* for a scholar. Although the instrumentation of *Jongmyo jeryeak* follows the general norms of the *aak* system, there are some characteristics that reveal the uniqueness of *Jongmyo jeryeak* : string instruments are included in both *deungga* and *heonga* ensembles; there is a *dochang* (導唱, lead singer); and the number of syllables in the texts varies, with 3 *eon* (three syllables), 4 *eon* (four syllables), or 5 *eon* (five syllables) per line.

The instrumentation of *Jongmyo jeryeak* was officially changed in 1463, when *Botaepyeong* and *Jeongdaeeop* were adopted as the ancestral ritual music. Subsequently, *Jongmyo jeryeak* underwent many reformations until settling into its current form. In the following, the historical changes of instrumentation in *Jongmyo jeryeak* are examined.

1) The Instrumentation of *Jongmyo jeryeak* in *Sejong sillok.*

In the early part of the Joseon Dynasty, *aak* was performed in *Jongmyo jerye*. The instrumentation, as recorded in *Sejong sillok*, is as of the time of King Taejong. The instrumentation of the *heonga* ensemble as given is somewhat

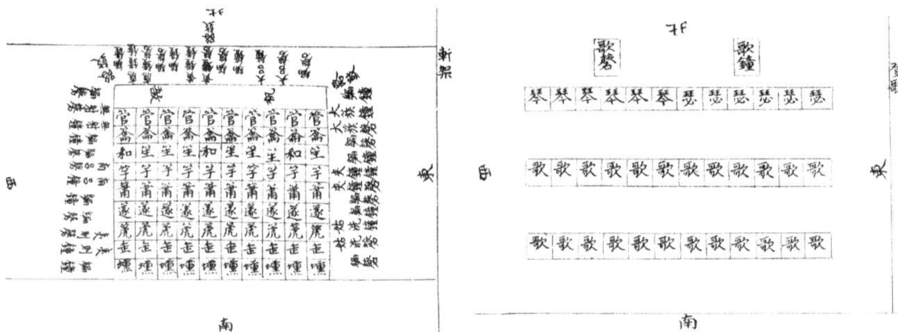

Figure 18. Arrangement of *heonga* (left) and *deungga* (right) ensembles in *Sejong sillok*

different from the instrumentation actually used in performance, since the eighteen *teukjong* and *teukgyeong* were not used.[2] After 1430 (the twelfth year of King Sejong's reign), the instrumentation was changed. Nevertheless, it remained similar to that of King Taejong, except that *jingo* and *nogo* were added to the *heonga* ensemble.[3]

During the time of King Sejong, *Jongmyo jeryeak* was still *aak*; the instrumentation also consisted of *aak* instruments, and the same instrumentation was used in rites for the god of wind, clouds, and thunderstorms, the god of agriculture, the god of sericulture, the god of rain, and Confucius. In other words, the orchestration of *Jongmyo jeryeak* was identical with that in other sacrificial rites.

2) *Sejong sillok* (*The Annals of King Sejong*) Vol. 43.27 and Vol. 47.12.

3) Yi Hye–gu, "Sejongjoui jongmyo jeryeak," in *Hanguk eumak seoseol*, (Seoul : Seoul daehakgyo chulpanbu, 1989), 157–161.

2) The Instrumentation of *Jongmyo jeryeak* in *Sejo sillok*

Before 1447 (the twenty–ninth year of King Sejong), new compositions–*Botaepyeong*, *Jeongdaeeop*, *Bongnaeui*, and *Balsang*–were created. From among these, *Botaepyeong* and *Jeongdaeeop* were chosen as *Jongmyo jeryeak* in 1463 (the ninth year of King Sejo's reign). There is no written record regarding the instrumentation of *Botaepyeong* and *Jeongdaeeop* during the time of King Sejong.[4] Accounts regarding the instrumentation of *Botaepyeong* and *Jeongdaeeop* after their adoption as *Jongmyo jeryeak* are found in *Sejo sillok* (1471); this instrumentation became the foundational system for *Jongmyo jeryeak* from that point on.

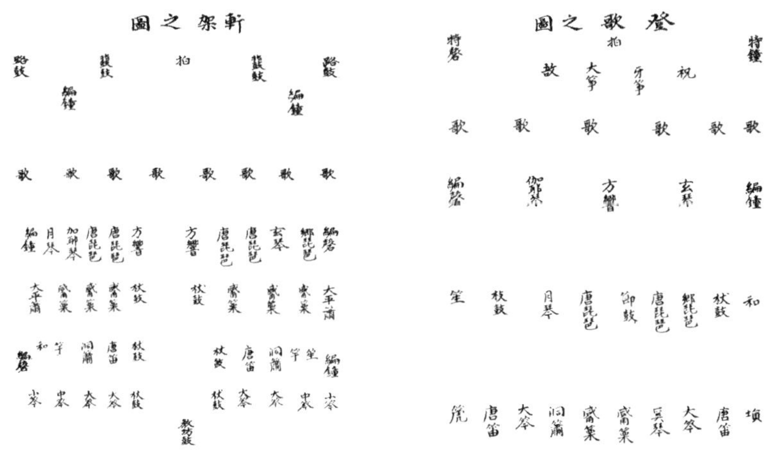

Figure 19. Arrangement of *heonga* (left) and *deungga* (right) ensembles in *Sejo sillok*

4) It is assumed that the instrumentation for *Botaepyeong* and *Jeongdaeeop* in the time of King Sejong would have followed that found in formal royal banquets; that instrumentation was recorded in *Sejong sillok*, vol. 65, in the sixteenth year of King Sejong's reign, on 18 August.

Comparing the instrumentation of *Jongmyo jeryeak*–which is indigenous Korean music–to that of *abu jeryeak* (Chinese–style court ritual music), the two have in common that both of them use *teukjong, teukgyeong, chuk, eo, jeolgo,* and singing. Nevertheless, they are different in that *abu jeryeak* uses *geum* and *seul*, whereas *Jongmyo jerye* applies *gayageum, hyeongeum, hyangbipa, dangbipa, ajaeng, daejaeng, wolgeum,* and *haegeum*–a mixture of *hyangak* and *dangak* instruments. In addition, only *Jongmyo jeryeak* utilizes percussion instruments such as *bak, banghyang, janggo,* and *gyobanggo.*

Regarding the *heonga* ensemble at the time of King Sejo, it is different from the ensemble that *abu jeryeak* used, including string instruments such as *gayageum, hyeongeum, hyangbipa, dangbipa, wolgeum,* and *haegeum*; and percussion instruments such as *bak, banghyang, janggo,* and *gyobanggo*; together with singing.

3) The Instrumentation of *Jongmyo jeryeak* in *Gukjooryeui* (1474)

The instrumentation found in *Gukjooryeui* demonstrates a transitional form that existed between the time of King Sejo and the publication of *Akhakgwebeom* (樂學軌範, *Guide to the Study of Music*, 1493). The compilation of *Sejo sillok* began in 1469 and was completed in 1471, while *Gukjooryeui* was published in 1474. Even though *Gukjooryeui* was published slightly later, one might say they were issued at about the same time. Nevertheless, while the *deungga* ensemble kept the same configuration, the *heonga* ensemble displays some differences between the two. In the *heonga* ensemble, in particular,

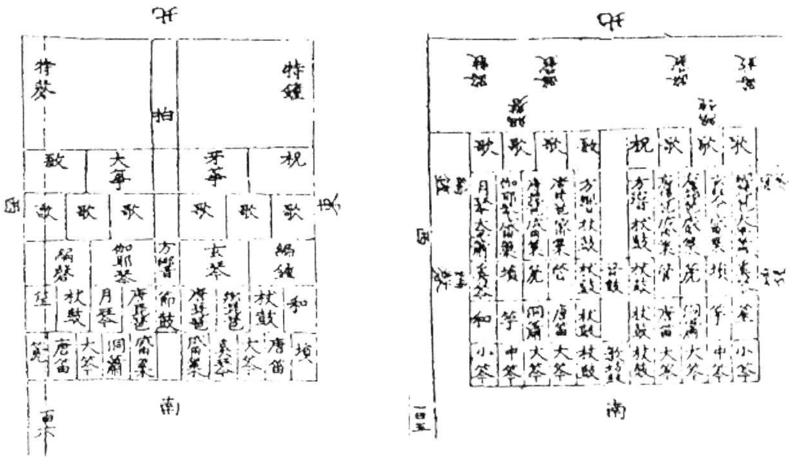

Figure 20. Arrangement of *deungga* (left) and *heonga* (right) ensembles in *Gukjooryeui*

the location and direction of the *pyeonjong* and the *pyeongyeong* were changed. In *Sejo sillok,* these instruments were located within the rectangular configuration of instruments arranged facing north, whereas in *Gukjooryeui,* they were placed outside of that configuration, facing inward. In addition, *Gukjooryeui* includes two *haegeum,* two *hun,* two *ji,* two *gwan,* and two *janggu.* Furthermore, in *Sejo sillok,* the *heonga* ensemble does not contain *chuk, eo,* or *jingo,* in contrast to *Gukjooryeui,* which includes those instruments in its instrumentation. The directions of *nogo* and *nodo* were changed from facing north to facing south.

4) The Instrumentation of *Jongmyo jeryeak* in *Akhakgwebeom*(1493)

The instrumentation recorded in *Akhakgwebeom* is an exemplary model. Even though the *Jongmyo jeryeak* instrumentation in *Akhakgwebeom* is the same as that in *Gukjooryeui*, the location and direction of the instruments are different. In the *heonga* ensemble, there was a slight change, compared to *Gukjooryeui*, in which the directions of *nogo*, *nodo*, *pyeonjong* and *pyeongyeong* were facing outward. Meanwhile, in the *deungga* ensemble, *pyeonjong* and *pyeongyeong*–which were located in the middle of the instrument configuration in *Gukjooryeui*–were pushed back to the southernmost row. In addition, *daegaeng* and *ajaeng* were located with other string instruments, and percussion instruments such as *chuk*, *eo*, *teukjong*, and *teukgyeong* were set together in the same row.

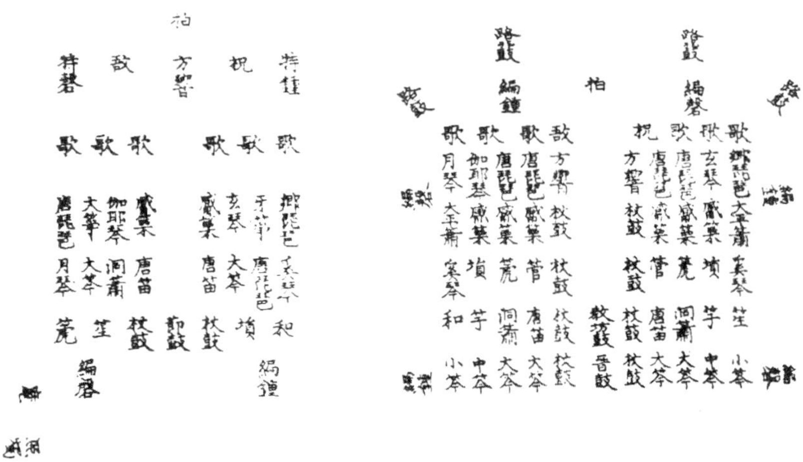

Figure 21. Arrangement of *deungga* (left) and *heonga* (right) ensembles in *Akhakgwebeom*

5) The Instrumentation of *Jongmyo jeryeak* in *Jongmyouigwe*(1706)

The first record of the instrumentation of *Jongmyo jeryeak* after the Imjinwaeran is found in the *Jongmyouigwe*, a collection of four books. The number of instruments used in the *deungga* ensemble decreases to sixteen, compared to the *Akhakgwebeom* which lists twenty–six instruments. In the *heonga* ensemble, wind instruments such as *saeng*, *u*, *hwa*, *gwan*, and *ji* were disused, as were string instruments such as *gayageum* and *geomungo*. Further, *teukjong*, *teukgyeong*, and *nogo* were no longer included.

The most distinct change in *Jongmyouigwe* is seen in the use of instruments in the *heonga* ensemble that had been used as dance implements in "Jeongdaeeopjimu." *Akhakgwebeom* records thirty–five people holding these implements, besides the thirty–six *ilmu* dancers in *Jeongdaeeop* performance. Included among these dance implements were musical instruments, such as *daegak* (大角, large horn), *nagak* (螺角, conch shell), *buk* (barrel drum), *daegeum* (大金, large gong), and *sogeum* (小金, small gong). In *Jongmyouigwe*, these implements are mostly absent, with the exception of *geom*, *chang*, and *gungsi* used by *ilmu* dancers, and the small and large gongs included in the *heonga* ensemble. In fact, in the latter work the small and large gongs do not have separate players, but are played by *akjang* singers. In other words, compared to *Akhakgwebeom*, the instrumentation in *Jongmyouigwe* has been downsized, and some dance implements have become musical instruments.

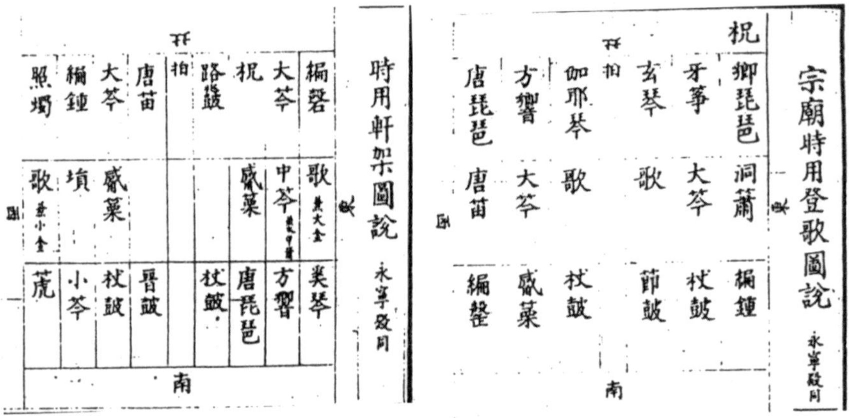

Figure 22. Arrangement of *heonga* (left) and *deungga* (right) ensembles in *Jongmyouigwe*

6) The Instrumentation of *Jongmyo jeryeak* in *Chungwantonggo* (1788)

Chungwantonggo is a resource that details the instrumentation of *Jongmyo jeryeak* in the eighteenth century. Compared to *Jongmyouigwe*, the distinctive feature of *Chungwantonggo* is the omission of *junggeum* and *sogeum* from the *samjuk* (三竹, lit. "three bamboo," indicating *daegeum, junggeum,* and *sogeum*). Of these three instruments, only the *daegeum* was included in all court music ensembles. At the time of *Gukjooryeui*, the *junggeum* and *sogeum* were part of the instrumentation of *Jongmyo jeryeak* and other court music. By the time of *Akhakgwebeom*, the two instruments were used only in *Jongmyo jeryeak*, and eventually, they were omitted from *Jongmyo jeryeak* in the period of *Chungwantonggo*.

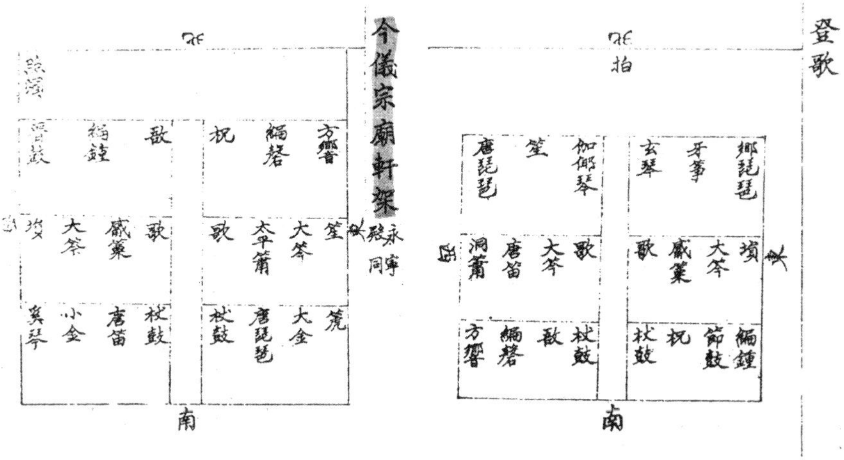

Figure 23. Arrangement of *heonga* (left) and *deungga* (right) ensembles in *Chungwantonggo*

7) The Instrumentation of *Jongmyo jeryeak* in 1892

Revised instrumentation for *Jongmyo jeryeak* was presented in 1892, in *Joseonakgaeyo* (朝鮮樂概要, *Summary of the Music of the Joseon Dynasty*).[5] The year of 1892 was the fifth observance of *imjinnyeon* (壬辰年, the year of imjin)[6] since the Imjinwaeran, the Japanese invasion of Korea in 1592. In that year, many national events–such as the dedication of the eulogistic posthumous title to King Seonjo, and rite for King Sinjong (神宗) of the Ming Dynasty in China who dispatched troops to defend Joseon from the Japanese invasion–

5) *Joseonakgaeyo* was written by Ham Hwa–jin (1884–1948) in 1917. Ham was a royal musician and from a family of royal musicians in the Joseon Dynasty. The book presents the instrumentation of *Jongmyo jeryeak* in 1892 as well as the current (1917) instrumentation. Ham wrote the book for submission to the Imperial Household Agency of Japan.

6) A year calculated by the sexagenary cycle that sets sixty years as a complete cycle.

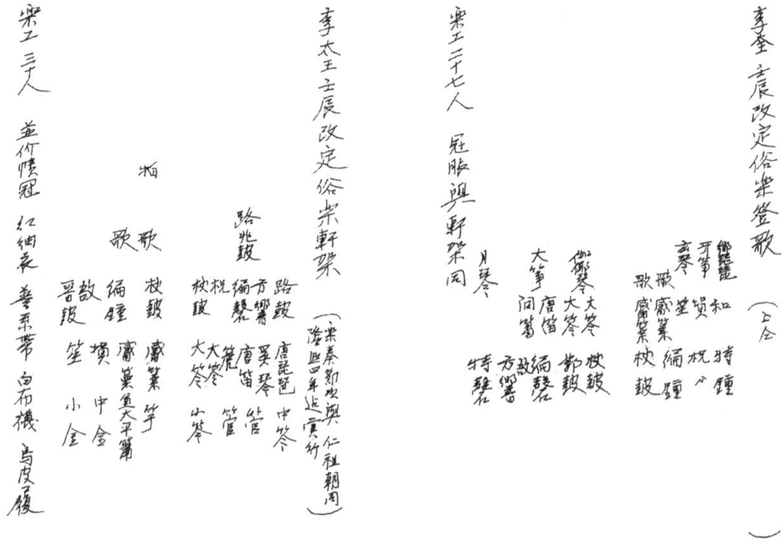

Figure 24. Revised arrangement (1892) of *heonga* (left) and *deungga* (right) ensembles in *Joseonakgaeyo*

were held. Besides these activities, the music system was also revised, and revised instrumentation for *Jongmyo jeryeak* is included in *Joseonakgaeyo*. In the revised instrumentation, *junggeum* and *sogeum*, which had been omitted since the time of *Chungwantonggo*, are included. The revised instrumentation was maintained until the time of the Korean Empire.

8) The Instrumentation of *Jongmyo jeryeak* in *Daehanyejeon* (1898)

Daehanyejeon (大韓禮典, *Code of Courtesy of the Korean Empire*) was written by Jang Ji-yeon (1864–1921). The instrumentation of *Jongmyo jeryeak* in *Daehanyejeon* is very similar to that in *Joseonakgaeyo*, in that *junggeum* and

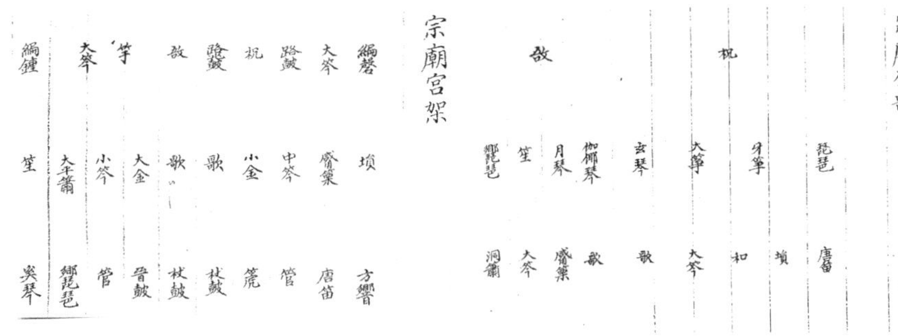

Figure 25. Arrangement of *gungga* (left) and *deungga* (right) ensembles in *Daehanyejeon*

sogeum are included in the *heonga* ensemble. The music system recorded in the book presents the alterations introduced : the use of *parilmu* with sixty–four dancers in eight lines, and the name change of the *heonga* ensemble to the *gungga* ensemble, so as to adopt the status of an empire. However, except for the use of larger–scale *ilmu*, it is hard to say that the instrumentation of *Jongmyo jeryeak* was properly adjusted to a standard appropriate for an empire.

9) The Instrumentation of *Jongmyo jeryeak* during the Japanese Colonial Period (1910–1945)

The instrumentation of *Jongmyo jeryeak* was changed once again when the nation was annexed to Japan. According to the *Jongmyo jeryeak* instrumentation from *Joseonakgaeyo* of 1917, ten kinds of instruments were included in the *deungga* ensemble : *bak, ajaeng, piri, daegeum, pyeonjong, pyeongyeong, banghyang, jeolgo, janggu,* and *chuk*. The *heonga* ensemble consisted of twelve kinds of instruments : *bak, chuk, piri, daegeum, haegeum, taepyeongso, pyeonjong, pyeongyeong, banghyang, jingo, janggu,* and *jing*. In other words, the instrumentation of *Jongmyo jeryeak* during the Japanese colonial period consisted of only its basic structure.

As mentioned above, the *Jongmyo jeryeak* instrumentation established during the Japanese colonial period has been maintained until today, with small changes. The *ilmu* was changed to the larger size of *parilmu*, and *eo* was added to the *deungga* and *heonga* ensembles. Also, regarding the number of instruments used in the ensembles, multiple *daegeum*, *piri*, and *haegeum* are included, although their numbers are not fixed. Meanwhile, all the percussion instruments are singly represented.

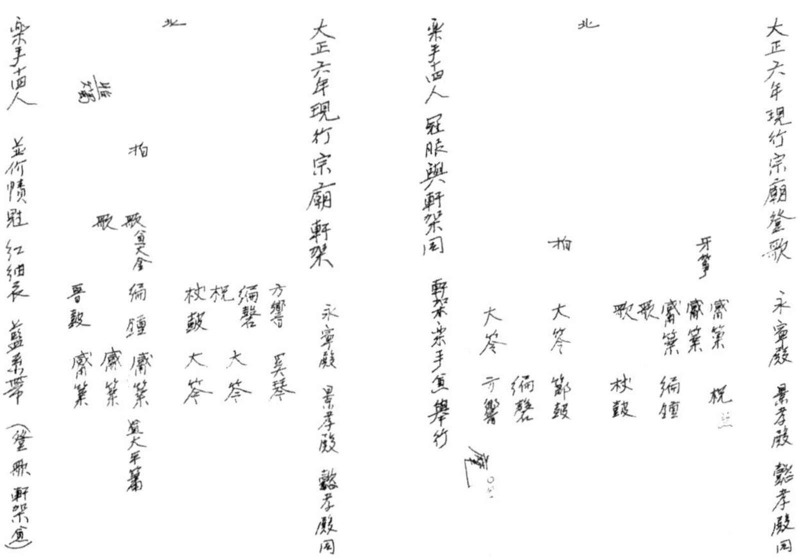

Figure 26. Arrangement (1917) of *heonga* (left) and *deungga* (right) ensembles in *Joseonakgaeyo*

The most distinctive characteristic of the instrumentation in *Jongmyo jeryeak* is the use of the three bamboo flutes, *daegeum*, *junggeum*, and *sogeum*. These indigenous Korean instruments have been used since the Silla Kingdom (新羅, 57 BC–AD 935). In this regards, *Jongmyo jeryeak* is a music faithfully carrying on the traditions of the Korean people. Another characteristic of *Jongmyo jeryeak* is the use of *taepyeongso*, an instrument used in military camps. Among court music genres, *Jongmyo jeryeak* is the only one to apply *taepyeongso*.

The changes of instrumentation for *Jongmyo jeryeak* have been recorded over hundreds of years since the adoption of *Botaepyeong* and *Jeongdaeeop* as *Jongmyo jeryeak* in 1464. Although the original instrumentation of *Jongmyo jeryeak* consisted of a splendid combination of all the string, wind, and percussion instruments, the current roster follows the downsized instrumentation developed during the Japanese colonial period.

2. The Procedure of the Ritual and its Music

Today, the overall structure of *Jongmyo jerye* consists of Singwan-rye, Cheonjo-rye (薦俎禮, offering the sacrifices), Choheon-rye, Aheon-rye, Jongheon-rye, Eumbok-rye, Cheolbyeondu, and Mangnyo-rye. The specific procedures in which the music is performed are Yeongsin, Jeonpye, Jinchan, Choheon, Aheon, Jongheon, Cheolbyeondu, and Songsin.

1) "Yeongsinhuimun" in Yeongsin

Yeongsin is the procedure of welcoming the gods. Today, the procedure is practiced as part of the Singwan–rye, the ritual of calling spirits at dawn which includes burning incense to call spirits in heaven, pouring wine to call spirits in earth, and offering gifts. The Yeongsin procedure begins when the musicians and dancers are in their positions, the ancestral tablets are set in their places, and the king, in his full ritual costume holding a scepter in his hands, stands in the *panwi* after entering through the main gate.

In the procedure, "Yeongsinhuimun" is played by the *heonga* ensemble and the *ilmu* is *munmu*, the civil dance. "Yeongsinhuimun" utilizes the same melody as "Huimun" from *Botaepyeong*, but the two texts are different. "Yeongsinhuimun" is performed nine times (usually referred to as "*guseong*" (九成, lit. "achieve nine times")).[7] At the beginning of the eighth playing of the piece, when the *aksa*(樂師, leader of the *akgong* or the *aksaeng*, usually senior musicians) asks for "*bureuo*" (chant), the *alja* chants "*bureuo*." Immediately after listening to the *alja*'s announcement, as the *jiprye* reads the *holgi*, chanting "heongwan iha gaesabae" (all officiants bow four times except the priests), the officiants bow four times. In the same manner, on the ninth playing of the piece, the ending of the music is announced with chanting. In fact, today, the piece is not performed nine times. Regarding the *ilmu* as well, while "Botaepyeongjimu" should be performed nine times, it is not, because the

7) The reason for performing the piece nine times is that *Jongmyo jerye* is a rite for human spirits. By contrast, in rites for heavenly spirits, the music is performed six times; in rites for earthly spirits, eight times.

manner of performing the ritual was changed.

2) "Jeonpyehuimun" in Jeonpye

Jeonpye is also part of Singwan–rye. As mentioned above, Singwan–rye includes a gift–offering procedure; this is Jeonpye, in which the gift, called *pyebaek*–a piece of white ramie cloth–is presented to the spirits. During the procedure, the *deungga* ensemble plays "Jeonpyehuimun" with the *ilmu*, "Botaepyeongjimu." Although the melody line of "Jeonpyehuimun" is the same as that of "Yeongsinhuimun," its tempo is much slower than that of "Yeongsinhuimun." However, it is believed that the tempo of "Jeonpyehuimun" was originally not as slow as it is today, but rather that the music was altered to fit into the ritual process; according to some written documents such as *Akhakgwebeom*, the musical piece in the Jeonpye procedure was named "Huimun." Seong Gyeon–rin (成慶麟, 1911–2008) states that the Jeonpye procedure was completed as the musicians played "Huimun" twice in slow tempo.[8)]

3) "Punganjiak" in Jinchan

Jinchan is also called Cheonjo–rye (薦俎禮) because it is the procedure of offering sacrificial meats on the *jo*. When the *jo* enters the gate, the *heonga* ensemble performs "Punganjiak," which does not belong to *Botaepyeong* nor to

8) Seong Gyeong–rin, 1977. *Gugak gamsang* (Seoul : Samho chulpansa).

Jeongdaeeop, but rather is a piece in *aak* style. The reason for using "Punganjiak" in *aak* style, instead of playing *Botaepyeong* or *Jeongdaeeop* which accompany dance, is because the Jinchan procedure follows the ritual tradition of the Chinese Song Dynasty, which does not include an accompanying dance.[9] When presentation of the sacrificial meats is complete, the music ends. There is no fixed number of repetitions, but in general it takes six to seven iterations of the piece before the Jinchan procedure is completed.

"Punganjiak" uses a scale of seven tones : Hwang (黃, C), Tae (太, D), Go (姑, E), Jung (仲, F), Im (林, G), Nam (南, A), and Eung (應, B).[10] However, it is not wrong to say that the piece is in the *cheonghwangjonggung pyeongjo* (淸黃鐘宮平調, *pyeongjo* mode with Hwangjong in the higher octave as a central tone) mode, as is *Botaepyeong*. In fact, in *Akhakgwebeom*, the piece is declared to be in the mode of *cheonghwangjonggung pyeongjo*.[11] The piece begins and also ends with Hwang (C). Regarding notation, the music is written in both Oeumyakbo (五音略譜, 5–tone abridged notation) and Gongcheokbo (工尺譜, simplified–character notation); parts that it is not possible to notate in Oeumyakbo are written in Gongcheokbo.

9) *Sejo sillok* (*The Annals of King Sejo*) Vol. 48.a5.

10) The full names of the twelve pitches in the chromatic scale are : Hwangjong (黃鐘, C), Daeryeo (大呂, C$^{\#}$) Taeju (太簇, D), Hyeopjong (夾鐘, E$^{\flat}$), Goseon (姑洗, E), Jungryeo (仲呂, F), Yubin (蕤賓, F$^{\#}$), Imjong (林鐘, G), Ichik (夷則, G$^{\#}$), Namryeo (南呂, A), Muyeok (無射, A$^{\#}$), and Eungjong (應鍾, B). For pitch notation, only the first character of each pair is used. Also, English pitch names do not specifically indicate the pitches in a certain musical register since each instrument has different pitch ranges. However, some pitches are marked with special signs–for example, "C',"implying an octave lower pitch than C used when necessary.

11) Refer to "Siyongsokbujeak jongmyo" in *Akhakgwebeom* Vol. 2.

4) "Botaepyeongjiak" in Choheon

When the king, as an officiant for the first wine offering, stands at the *junso* of the first chamber facing west, the *deungga* ensemble plays *Botaepyeong* accompanying the *ilmu* of civil dance. *Botaepyeong* is a musical suite consisting of eleven pieces : "Huimun," "Gimyeong," "Gwiin," "Hyeongga," "Jipnyeong," "Yunghwa," "Hyeonmi," "Yonggwang–Jeongmyeong," "Junggwang," "Daeyu," and "Yeokseong." The first piece, "Huimun," is performed when the officiant goes into the chamber, and "Yeokseong," the last piece, is played for exiting the chamber.

When the *jipsa* says "*deuo*" (lit. "hold up"), the ensemble plays "Iniphuimun."[12] The king goes to the *junso* and waits. When the *jipsa* tells the *jiprye* that "Iniphuimun" is finished and the second piece, "Gimyeong," is playing, the *jiprye* tells the king to proceed to the ancestral tablets in the first chamber. The music stops, and the king sits kneeling after offering the first wine. When the *daechuk* finishes reading the written prayer, the *jeolgo* is performed three times, followed by the *bak* played once, and the music continues.

The king moves on to the second chamber, and performs the same ritual as in the first chamber, repeating it until he finishes the offering in the nineteenth chamber. Meanwhile, the musicians perform music continuously from "Gimyeong" to "Daeyu" until the *daechuk* finishes reading the written

12) "Iniphuimun" refers to "Huimun." The "Huimun" playing during the officiant's entrance into the chamber is also called "Iniphuimun," since *inip* means "to lead something inside."

prayer in the nineteenth chamber. When the last prayer reading is over, the musicians play "Inchul–Yeokseong."[13] After the king goes back to his position, the *jipsa* waits until the piece is over, and orders the music to end.

During the first wine offering, musicians, especially *bak*, *pyeonjong*, and *piri* players, have to be alert to the action, as there are frequent pauses in the music because of the prayer readings. Today, however, as separate officiants are assigned for each chamber, the whole of *Botaepyeong* does not need to be performed. After performing "Iniphuimun," musicians repeat "Gimyeong" and "Gwiin," and when the procedure is done, they move on to playing "Inchul–Yeokseong."

5) "Jeongdaeeopjiak" in Aheon

When the *aheongwan* goes to the *junso* of the first chamber, and stands facing west, the *heonga* ensemble plays *Jeongdaeeop* accompanying the *ilmu* of military dance. *Jeongdaeeop* consists of eleven pieces : "Somu," "Dokgyeong," "Takryeong," "Seonwi," "Sinjeong," "Bunung," "Suneung," "Chongsu," "Jeongse," "Hyeokjeong," and "Yeonggwan." During the procedure of the second wine offering, the reading of written prayers is omitted so that the musicians play the music from "Dokgyeong" to "Hyeokjeong" repeatedly without ceasing until the *aheongwan* finishes the second wine offering in the nineteenth chamber. When the *aheongwan* comes out of the last chamber,

13) "Inchul–Yeokseong" refers to "Yeokseong," the last piece of *Botaepyeong*. Forming a counterpart to "Iniphuimun," "Inchul–Yeokseong" is played during the officiant's retreat from the chamber, as *inchul* means "pulling out."

the *jipsa* holds *deung* (a lamp) up high signaling the musicians to perform "Inchul–Yeonggwan."[14] When the *aheongwan* returns to his position, the *jipsa* waits until the piece is over, and orders the music to end.

Because the primary purpose of the music is to accompany the ritual, the duration of the performance is decided by the length of the procedure. Other than the first and last pieces, which serve to accompany the advance and retreat of the officiant, the remaining pieces in between are played in order, yet can be stopped at any piece if the procedure is over, or are repeatedly performed until the procedure is done, as was mentioned above. Whichever piece is being performed when the *jipsa* holds up the *deung*, the musicians then play the last piece, "Yeonggwan." If the music is repeated and "Bunung" is played again, *taepyeongso* is omitted and only *piri* is used.

Jeongdaeeop in Aheon begins with *Jingosiptong* (晉鼓十通, beating *jingo* ten times), followed with the playing of the *chuk*, *jingo*, and *bak*, in the same way as for the *akjak* (樂作, the beginning of music) of *Botaepyeong*. For *akji*(樂止, the ending of music), *bak*, *jingo*, and *eo* are played.

6) "Jeongdaeeopjiak" in Jongheon

The Jongheon procedure is executed in the same manner as Aheon. The *heonga* ensemble performs the eleven pieces of *Jeongdaeeop*, with military dance *ilmu*. Unlike Aheon, though, Jongheon begins with Jingosamtong (晉

14) A reference to "Yeonggwan," the last piece of *Jeongdaeeop*. In the same manner as with *Botaepyeong*, the last piece of *Jeongdaeeop* is performed during the retreat of the officiant from the chamber; it is called "Inchul–Yeonggwan."

鼓三通, beating *jingo* three times) following by *bak*. As the end of the music is marked by *Daegeumsipcha* (大金十次, beating the large gong ten times), the music and dance end together.

7) "Onganjiak" in Cheolbyeondu

During the procedure of Cheolbyeondu, "Onganjiak" is performed. There is no dance performance in Cheolbyeondu, following the practice of the Song Dynasty in China. "Onganjiak" is the same music as "Punganjiak" in Jinchan; however, "Punganjiak" in Jinchan is played by the *heonga* ensemble whereas "Onganjiak" in Cheolbyeondu is performed by the *deungga* ensemble. The *akjak* and *akji* of "Onganjiak" are the same as those in "Yeongsinhuimun."

8) "Heunganjiak" in Songsin

"Heunganjiak" is played by the *heonga* ensemble. As in Jinchan, only music without dancing is performed, following the Song Dynasty practice. The melody of "Heunganjiak" is the same as that of "Punganjiak" in Jinchan, but the texts are different. The *akjak* and *akji* of "Heunganjiak" are the same as those in "Yeongsinhuimun."

3 . Music Scores and Musical Features

The music scores and musical features of *Jongmyo jeryeak* will be discussed under following themes : types and features of scores, the beginnings and endings of music, and musical features including scales and rhythm.

1) The Music Scores for *Jongmyo jeryeak*

Jongmyo jeryeak of the Joseon Dynasty traversed four great stages over its history. First, earlier Goryeo music was played with slight alterations. The second period is when *Jongmyo jeryeak* was rearranged based on Im U's *Daeseongakbo* (大晟樂譜); the third stage was marked by the adoption of *Botaepyeong* and *Jeongdaeeop* as *Jongmyo jeryeak* during King Sejo's reign; and the fourth arrived when "Junggwang" was added to *Botaepyeong* during King Injo's reign. *Jongmyo jeryeak* in its present form, with *Botaepyeong* and *Jeongdaeeop* at its core, is found in *Sejo sillok*, *Daeakhubo* (大樂後譜), *Akjangyoram* (樂章要覽), and *Sogagwonbo* (俗樂源譜). There are also versions rendered in Jeongganbo (井間譜, Korean mensural notation) and western staff notation, created after the founding of Gungnipgugagwon (National Gugak Center).

The music scores for *Jongmyo jeryeak* indicate two musical aspects–pitch and time value. Pitch is recorded in three ways : Oeumyakbo (五音略譜), a combination of Oeumyakbo and Yulja (律字, music letter), and Yulja alone. Time values are indicated in three styles : Jeongganbo with six *daegang* (groups of *jeonggan*) per column, in the pattern of 3 · 2 · 3 · 3 · 2 · 3 *jeonggan* (a set of squares representing a rhythmic unit) grouping; another *Jeongganbo* in six *daegang* form, but, in reality, not following the time value; and notation only using Yulja. The characteristics of these notation systems are discussed below.

(1) Music Scores in *Sejo sillok*.

Botaepyeong and *Jeongdaeeop* were newly–composed during King Sejong's time, with the intention that they be used at public and private banquets. During King Sejong's reign, *Botaepyeong* consisted of eleven musical pieces, while *Jeongdaeeop* comprised fifteen. Both were recorded in the 138th volume of *Sejong sillok*. The music scores of *Botaepyeong* and *Jeongdaeeop* in *Sejong sillok* are in Jeongganbo using thirty–two *jeonggan* per column. In King Sejo's time, *Botaepyeong* and *Jeongdaeeop* were included in *Jongmyo jeryeak*, with alterations in the number of musical pieces, titles, length, and lyrics. As it became ritual music, the number of musical pieces in each was reduced to eleven. Moreover, *Botaepyeong*, originally in *imjong pyeongjo* mode, was changed to *cheonghwangjong pyeongjo*, and *Jeongdaeeop*, originally in *namryeo gyemyeonjo* mode, was also transposed to *cheonghwangjong pyeongjo*. In addition, the length of the music and the lyrics were partly altered to suit the ritual process. This is recorded in the 48th volume of *Sejo sillok*.

After incorporation of *Botaepyeong* and *Jeongdaeeop* into *Jongmyo jeryeak*, the music of *Jongmyo jeryeak* in *Sejo sillok* is recorded in Jeongganbo using the six *daegang* system of 3 · 2 · 3 · 3 · 2 · 3 *jeonggan* grouping. Examining the music in *Sejo sillok*, in the case of *Jongmyo jeryeak*, pitch is indicated using Oeumyakbo and time value is illustrated with *jeonggan*. As exceptions,

"Heunganjiak" of Jinhan, "Onganjiak" of Cheolbyeondu, and "Heunganjiak" of Songsin all use the heptatonic scale, and employ Gongcheokbo for pitches that cannot be indicated using Oeumyakbo.

(2) *Daeakhubo*

After Imjinwaeran, in the fourth year of King Injo (1626), "Junggwang" was added to *Botaepyeong* to commemorate the deeds of royal ancestors. Then, "Yonggwang" and "Jeongmyeong" were combined to become "Yonggwang–Jeongmyeong," in order to keep the number pieces in *Botaepyeong* at eleven. Also, according to *Jongmyouigwe*, published in 1706, the instrumentation and dances of *Jongmyo jeryeak* underwent great change in the eighteenth century. Although *Daeakhubo* was compiled in 1759 (the thirty–fifth year of King Yeongjo's reign), it contains music from King Sejo's time, and recorded *Jongmyo jeryeak* from *Sejo sillok* with little change. However, it displays some musical changes. First, it includes the added "Junggwang" piece, and "Yonggwang" and "Jeongmyeong" are recorded as a single piece. Second, in terms of notating pitch, while music scores in *Sejo sillok* are in Oeumyakbo, *Daeakhubo* uses both Oeumyakbo and Yulja at the same time. Third, *Sejo sillok* uses Gongcheokbo for notes, Goseon (E) and Eungjong (B) appearing in "Punganjiak," "Onganjiak," and "Heunganjiak," whereas *Daeakhubo* renders these notes using Oeumyakbo, as "下一界" or "下四界". Although *Daeakhubo* is significant in that it is the first record including the added "Junggwang" after Imjinwaeran, as well as the unified "Yonggwang–Jeongmyeong" piece, it offers little more than the previous *Jongmyo jeryeak* as contained in *Sejo sillok*, with no hint about the actual *Jongmyo jeryeak* performed at the time.

(3) *Akjangyoram*

Akjangyoram is an anonymous script, published before 1829, which contains *gayageum* and *geomungo* parts in *Jongmyo jeryeak*. *Geomungo* and *gayageum* were originally used in both the *deungga* and *heonga* ensembles of *Jongmyo jeryeak*. However, these instruments were already omitted from the *deungga* ensemble in *Jongmyouigwe* and, although said to have been used until the instrumentation renovation of 1892, they were omitted from the *heonga* ensemble by the year 1917.

The method of notation used in *Akjangyoram* is Yuljabo (律字譜, music letter notation); when note duration exceeds a single beat, a dot is notated below Yulja. *Akjangyoram* can be said to be the first notation which indicates rhythmic change, using Yuljabo rather than Jeongganbo. In other words, instead of indicating melodic rhythm by word composition in the lyrics, as in previous sources, *Akjangyoram* uses a system in which each note is consistently one or two beats. Another outstanding feature is that it indicates "Gyeokdobeop" (擊挑法), a playing method especially designed for *gayageum* and *geomungo*. The music of *Jongmyo jeryeak* notated in Yuljabo as contained in *Akjangyoram* is still being used today as notation for *pyeonjong*, *pyeongyeong*, *daegeum*, *piri*, and *haegeum*.

(4) *Sogagwonbo*

Sogagwonbo was compiled as part of the instrumentation renovation conducted in the Imjin year of 1892. In *Sogagwonbo, Jongmyo jeryeak* appears in the Inpyeon (仁篇) section of volume 1 and the Sinpyeon (信篇) section of volume 6. In the former, the music is identical to that contained in *Daeakhubo* in that it uses Oeumyakbo and Yulja, as well as the notated order of lyrics, beats, and *janggu* patterns, but differs in the placement of lyrics. This indicates that *Inpyeon* of *Sogagwonbo*, rather than recording *Jongmyo jeryeak* as performed at the time, is merely a copy of *Jongmyo jeryeak* as contained in *Daeakhubo*, with slight inconsistencies resulting from copying errors. In *Sinpyeon* in volume 6, there is music for *geomungo, gayageum*, and *bipa*. The notation uses six *daegang* with 3 · 2 · 3 · 3 · 2 · 3 *jeonggan* grouping in Jeongganbo, which, however, has little meaning, and the entire notation is rather more similar to Yuljabo. In its musical contents, it is identical to *Jongmyo jeryeak* as contained in *Akjangyoram*. Another shared feature is the inclusion of Gyeokdobeop for stringed instruments. One difference is that *Akjangyoram* contains Gyeokdobeop for *gayageum* and *geomungo*, while the Gyeokdobeop in the *Sinpyeon* section of *Sogagwonbo* is for *gayageum, geomungo*, and *bipa*.

Jongmyo jeryeak in *Sejo sillok* and *Daeakhubo* take the form of a full score, while *Jongmyo jeryeak* as contained in the *Sinpyeon* section of *Sogagwonbo* notates music for the stringed instruments only : *gayageum, geomungo*, and *bipa*, recording instruments in the first row of previous music scores. Therefore, in terms of melodic features, it is little different from *Jongmyo jeryeak* recorded in *Sejo sillok*. But it already has no Yonggangbeop (用綱法), no distinction of *daegang*, and indicates no *rhythm* by word placement.

(5) Music Scores for *Jongmyo jeryeak* from the Japanese Occupation to the Present

Aakbu akbo (雅樂部樂譜) published in the 1930s contains no *Jongmyo jeryeak*. However, the *Yiwangjik aakbo* (李王職雅樂譜, Court Music Notation of the Yi Royal Family Bureau) stored in the Museum of Korean Music contains *Botaehwa* (保太和) and *Hyangmannyeon* (享萬年),[15] among the movements of *Jongmyo jeryeak*. But this was never published as a book, and we can therefore assume that official publication of *Jongmyo jeryeak* notation never took place during the Japanese colonial period. There was, however, music used personally by students for memorization, such as *Jeryejuaguiju* (祭禮奏樂儀註), which appears to have been hand–copied during the Yiwangjik aakbu (李王職雅樂部, Yi Royal Family Bureau of Court Music in the Japanese colonial era) period.

The National Gugak Center was founded after establishment of the Korean Republic, and published *Jongmyo jeryeak* in a music score entitled *Jongmyo jeryeak* in Jeongganbo notation in 1980; this was reissued in 2007, again using Jeongganbo. The music book, *Jongmyo jeryeak*, as part of the series on Korean music published by the Center, is in Jeongganbo using Yulja. However, it does not employ the six *daegang* system of 3 · 2 · 3 · 3 · 2 · 3, and its notational rules for *daegang* are scarcely consistent. Moreover, stringed instruments were notated as scores for *pyeonjong* and *pyeongyeong*. It also includes music for *daegeum*, *piri*, *haegeum*, *ajaeng*, and *akjang*, which had never

15) During the colonial period, the names of *Botaepyeong* and *Jeongdaeeop* were changed to *Botaehwa* and *Hyangmannyeon*, respectively.

been specifically recorded in the past. *Akjak* and *akji* parts are recorded in duple meter, and the main section of pieces are in triple meter.

Jongmyo jeryeak was transcribed into western staff notation during this period but never published. The first published staff notation was *Botaepyeong Jeongdaeeop*, as volume 11 of *Korean Music*, published by the National Gugak Center in 1973. This was revised in 2007 as *Jongmyo jeryeak*, volume 35 of *Korean Music*. In addition, instrumental versions of *Jongmyo jeryeak* were included in privately–published music scores. Some were in Jeongganbo and others were in Yuljabo.

Publishing only the lyrics could also be valuable, and there are many sources that record them. The words are written alongside music in books like *Sejo sillok*, *Daeakhubo*, the *Inpyeon* section of *Sogagwonbo*, and *Akjangyoram*, but there are also sources, such as *Akhakgwebeom*, *Akjanggasa*, *Jongmyouigwe*, *Chungwantonggo*, *Sogakgasa*, *Agwongosa*, and *Joseonakgaeyo*, which contain only the lyrics of *Jongmyo jeryeak*. In *Joseonakgaeyo*, however, lyrics newly–arranged in the Japanese colonial period were recorded. *Jongmyo jeryeak* published by the National Gugak Center in 1980 contains both sets of lyrics but its revision in 2007 returns to the original text, published as *Jongmyo jeryeak*, volume 18 of *Kugak jeonjip*. Another method of documenting the music is album production, and in 1980, the National Gugak Center released LP records containing entire movements of the ritual. In 1987, SKC sold compact discs with identical contents, and in 2007, the National Gugak Center released a CD of *Jongmyo jeryeak* as the 29th album of its Korean Music Series.

The *Jongmyo jeryeak* of the Joseon Dynasty clearly underwent changes to its musical contents, aside from formal alterations like the inclusion of "Junggwang" during King Injo's time and the conflation of "Yonggwang" and "Jeongmyeong." The various historical sources reflect those changes well.

2) *Akjak* and *Akji*, the Beginning and Ending of Music

Jongmyo jeryeak is music that accompanies a religious ritual and therefore has a beginning (*akjak*) and an ending (*akji*) for each procedure. It is often categorized as secular music, but its overall form follows the style of *aak*. So the beginnings and endings of *Jongmyo jeryeak* sound much like *aak* music, which largely comes in two styles–the style of *Botaepyeong* and that of *Jeongdaeeop*.

(1) *Akjak* and *Akji* in *Botaepyeong* Style

In the case of *Botaepyeong*, the *akjak* largely consist of Geohwi (擧麾, "deuo"), Gyeokbagilseong (擊拍一聲), Gochuksamseong (鼓柷三聲), and Gyeokgoiltong (擊鼓一通). When the *jipsa* chants "*deuo*" (hold up), the *bak* is struck once (Gyeokbagilseong) and the *chuk* is beaten three times (Gochuksamseong), followed by a single beat on the *buk* (Gyeokgoiltong). This pattern is repeated three times, concluded with another beat on the *bak*. For Choheon–rye, when the music starts after the reading of prayers, the *bak* is struck once more.

Movements that include *akjak* in *Botaepyeong* style are "Yeongsinhuimun," "Jeonpyehuimun," "Punganjiak" in Jinchan, *Botaepyeong* in Choheon,

"Onganjiak" in Cheolbyeondu, and "Heunganjiak" in Songsin. The *jeolgo* is played only in Gyeokgoiltong, "Jeonpyehuimun," *Botaepyeong* in Choheon, and "Onganjiak" in Cheolbyeondu played by the *deungga* ensemble, while for "Yeongsinhuimun," "Punganjiak" in Jinchan, and "Heunganjiak" in Songsin played by the *heonga* ensemble, *jingo* is used.

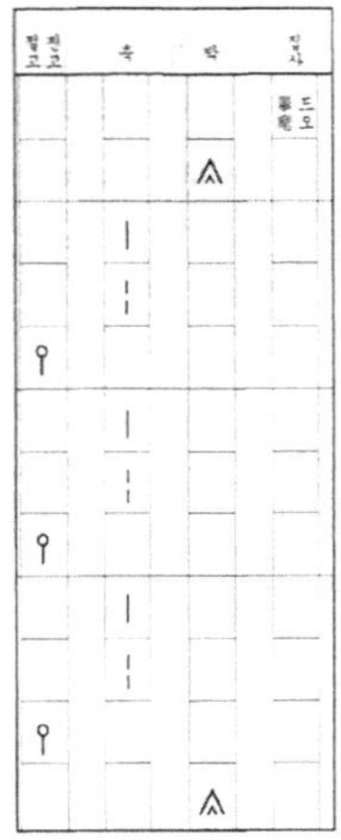

Figure 27. The *akjak* pattern in *Botaepyeong* style

The *akji* in the style of *Botaepyeong* begins as the *jipsa* calls out "*jio*" (偎䴥), followed by three beats on the *bak* and *buk*, respectively, with the *buk* half a beat later than the *bak*. The second repetition is accompanied by *eo*, when the wooden idiophone is scratched with a stick three times. The *deungga* ensemble plays *jeolgo* to end "Jeonpyehuimun," *Botaepyeong* in Choheon, and "Onganjiak" in Cheolbyeondu, and the *heonga* ensemble plays *jingo* for ending the movements of "Yeongsinhuimun," "Punganjiak" in Jinchan, and "Heunganjiak" in Songsin.

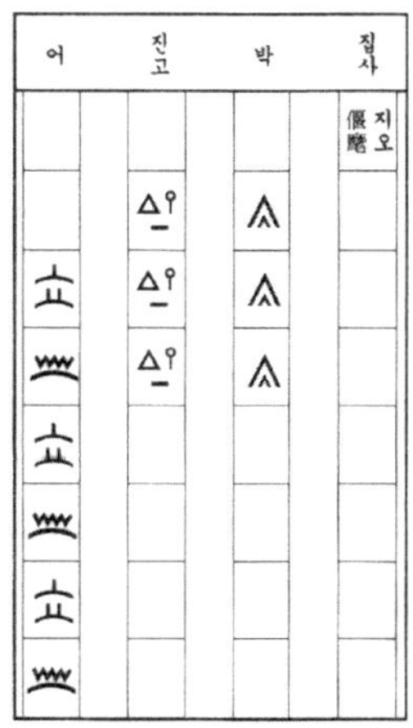

Figure 28. The *akji* pattern in *Botaepyeong* style

(2) *Akjak* and *Akji* in *Jeongdaeeop* Style

Jeongdaeeop is played during Aheon and Jongheon. For these procedures, the same music is played but with different beginnings and endings. The *akjak* of Aheon

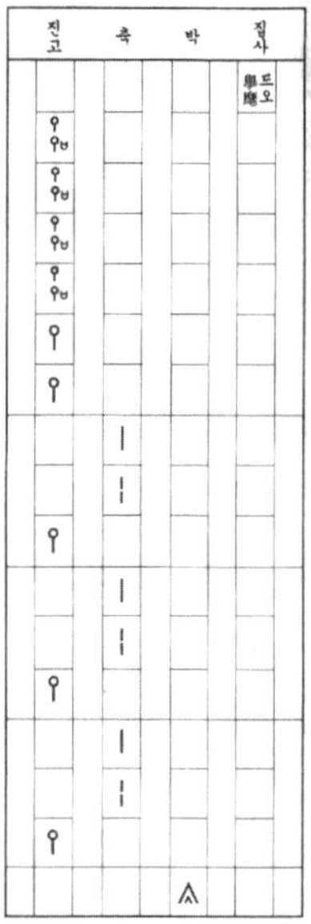

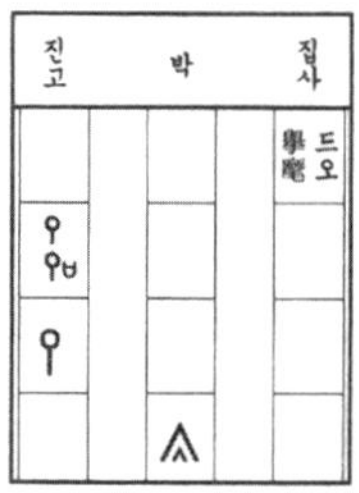

Figure 29 (left). The *akjak* pattern in Aheon
Figure 30 (right). The *akjak* pattern in Jongheon

in *Jeongdaeeop* starts when the *jipsa* calls out "*deuo*" and plays 10 beats on Jingosiptong (beating *jingo* ten times), followed by Gochuksamseong and Gyeokgoiltong, concluding with a single beat on the *bak*. In other words, what follows after Jingosiptong is identical to that in *Botaepyeong*. Meanwhile, in *Jeongdaeeop* of Jongheon, when the *jipsa* calls out "*deuo*," Jingosamtong and Gyeokbagilseong follow.

The *akji* for Aheon in *Jeongdaeeop* is the same as that in *Botaepyeong*. When the *jipsa* says "*jio*," *bak* and *buk* are struck three times, with the *buk* half a beat later than the *bak*. When this is repeated, the *eo* is played three times.

The *akji* for Jongheon in *Jeongdaeeop* is identical to that of Aheon in *Jeongdaeeop*, except for the addition of Daegeumsipcha. Here, the *jipsa* calls out "*jio*" and then the *bak* and *buk* (*jingo*) half a beat later, are struck three times. The second pattern is accompanied with *eo* and *daegeum* (large gong). The *daegeum* is played in its unique pattern, "jing jing– jing jing– jing jing– jing jing– jing– jing–," of ten beats while the *eo* plays a rhythmic pattern, "ttak– ttak ttak deu reu reu reu," repeated three times.

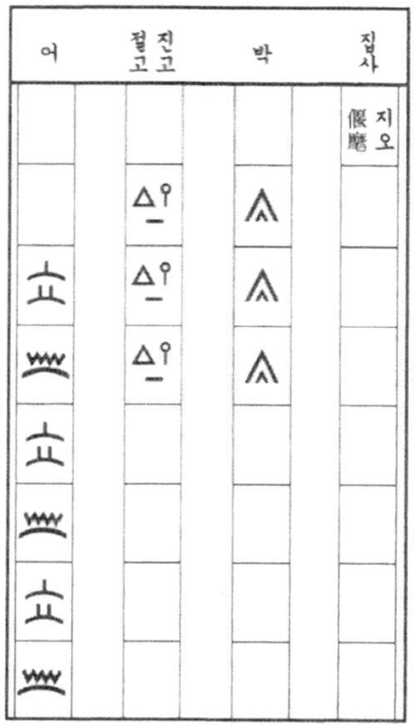

Figure 31. The *akji* pattern in Aheon

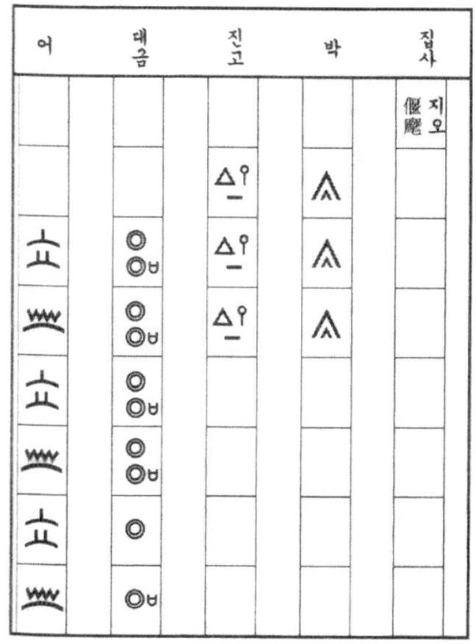

Figure 32. The *akji* pattern in Jongheon

Botaepyeong and *Jeongdaeeop* were composed based on *hyangak* and *gochwiak*, and although "Punganjiak," "Onganjiak," and "Heunganjiak" are in the form of *aak*, they are all presently in triple time. On the other hand, the *akjak* and *akji* are in duple time, since they follow the style of *aak*. Although beginnings and endings derive in form from *aak*, they are basically arrangements of secular music like *Botaepyeong* and *Jeongdaeeop*. Therefore, the *akjak* and *akji* are *aak* in form but *sogak* (indigenous Korean music) in musical content, and thus of complex nature. This is one of the major musical features of *Jongmyo jeryeak*.

3) Musical Features

Jongmyo jeryeak can be divided into *Botaepyeong*, *Jeongdaeeop*, and *Jinchanak* (進饌樂, music pieces used in Jinchan) styles. *Botaepyeong* style is played during Yeongsin, Jeonpye, and Choheon; *Jeongdaeeop* style is used during Aheon and Jongheon; and *Jinchanak*–style movements are employed for Jinchan, Cheolbyeondu, and Songsin procedures.

The eleven *Botaepyeong* pieces are "Huimun," "Gimyeong," "Gwiin," "Hyeongga," "Jimnyeong," "Yunghwa," "Hyeonmi," "Yonggwang-Jeongmyeong," "Junggwang," "Daeyu," and "Yeokseong." Among these, "Huimun" is played for Yeongsin, Jeonpye, and *inip* (officiant's entering the chamber) in Choheon, which are entitled "Yeongsinhuimun," "Jeonpyehuimun," and "Iniphuimun," respectively. "Yeongsinhuimun" and "Iniphuimun" are basically the same music with different lyrics, and while "Jeonpyehuimun," has different lyrics and tempo, its melodic flow is the same as that for "Yeongsinhuimun" and "Iniphuimun." "Yeokseong" and "Junggwang" are also the same, with different lyrics. When "Junggwang" was added during the fourth year of King Injo's reign, the lyrics were composed anew, while borrowing the melody of "Yeokseong" intact.

"Punganjiak" in Jinchan, "Onganjiak" in Cheolbyeondu, and "Heunganjiak" in Songsin all share the same melody, and were called *Jinchanak* in general. However, the term "Jinchan" merely refers to the ritual process. "Punganjiak," "Onganjiak," and "Heunganjiak" have the same melody, yet use different lyrics, and therefore should be considered as different pieces. What follows is a discussion on the musical features of *Jongmyo jeryeak*.

(1) Modes

Botaepyeong, including "Yeongsinhuimun" and "Jeonpyehuimun," employs *cheonghwangjong pyeongjo* as its mode. When *Botaepyeong* and *Jeongdaeeop* were included in the ritual process in the ninth year of King Sejo's reign, the previous *imjong pyeongjo* was changed to *cheonghwangjong pyeongjo* and has remained such ever since. The mode for *Jeongdaeeop* was originally *namryeo gyemyeonjo* but changed to *cheonghwangjong gyemyeonjo* in the ninth year of King Sejo's reign as it was included in *Jongmyo jeryeak*. At present, some of the instruments still follow the melodic form recorded in *Sejo sillok* while other instruments have changed mode.

The melodic line for stringed instruments in *Jeongdaeeop* as recorded in *Sejo sillok* is found intact in the melodies for *pyeonjong* and *pyeongyeong* today. In melodies for *piri, daegeum,* and *haegeum* in *Jeongdaeeop*, Hwangjong (C) tends to fall to Muyeok ($B^{b'}$), and Imjong (G) to Jungnyeo (F), which is analogous to melodies of *akjang*. However, the pitches in *akjang* underwent more changes than those for *piri, daegeum,* and *haegeum*. In the case of Hwangjong in the original *Jeongdaeeop, piri, daegeum,* and *haegeum* have not yet changed to Muyeok and still remain Hwangjong, while the melodies of *akjang* all turned to Muyeok. The melodic pattern of "Mu Hwang Mu Hwang" ($B^{b'}$–C–$B^{b'}$–C), a bridge from Hwangjong to Muyeok, is found more often in melodies for *piri, daegeum,* and *haegeum* than in *akjang*. In terms of the change from Im to Jung in *Jeongdaeeop*, *akjang* melodies have all changed from Im (G) to Jung (F), but for those in *piri*, *daegeum*, and *haegeum* parts, there are more cases of Im remaining the same.

The mode for *Jeongdaeeop* thus exists in three types : one, where the original melody is maintained, as in the case of *pyeonjong* and *pyeongyeong*; those which totally changed, as in *akjang*; and those in the middle ground, as for *piri*, *daegeum*, and *haegeum*. In general, the melody is either original or renewed. For example, melodies of *pyeonjong* and *pyeongyeong* in *Jeongdaeeop* are the same as those recorded in *Sejo sillok*, but among melodies of *piri*, *daegeum*, *haegeum* and *akjang*, Hwang (C) is changed to Mu ($B^{b'}$), and Im (G) is changed to Jung (F), resulting in the *pyeongjo* mode of Mu · Hwang · Hyeop · Jung · Im (B^{b}-C-Eb-F-G). Therefore, the *Jeongdaeeop* melody consists of Hwang · Hyeop · Jung · Im · Mu (C-E^{b}-F-G) and Mu · Hwang · Hyeop · Jung · Im (Bb-C-Eb-F-G) at the same time, making it sound rather dissonant.

Movements in *Jinchanak* style, including "Punganjiak," "Onganjiak," and "Heunganjiak," use a heptatonic mode : Hwang · Tae · Go · Jung · Im · Nam · Eung (C-D-E-F-G-A-B). However, since Goseon (E) and Eungjong (B) appear only once, one can scarcely consider them as part of the main scale. Therefore, we could say that this movement is in *cheonghwangjong pyeongjo*, as in *Botaepyeong*.

(2) Rhythms

In traditional Korean music, rhythm consists of rhythmic patterns called *jangdan*, accompanied by *janggu*. However, *Jongmyo jeryeak* lacks a consistent *janggu* pattern, and one can scarcely find an active rhythmic change in this music. Therefore, rhythm for *Jongmyo jeryeak* should be considered in terms of the rhythms of *bak*, melody, and text structures. The rhythm found in the *bak* means that the *bak* is struck on a regular cycle, and one could thereby study the rhythmic pattern according to where the *bak* is struck. The *bak* in *Jongmyo jeryeak* comes at the end of a text line. For pieces starting in the first and second *daegang*, *bak* occurs at the last syllable of a stanza, while for pieces beginning in the third *daegang*, it is struck at the end of *yoeum* (lingering sound) of *akjang* in every stanza. Today, we no longer have the musical form applying the *daegang* system, and therefore we cannot assert that *bak* is used at the end of every text line. "Gwiin," "Hyeongga," "Yunghwa," and "Yonggwang–Jeongmyeong" of *Botaepyeong*, and "Seonwi," "Takjeong," "Sinjeong," "Chongsu," "Jeongse," and "Yeonggwan" of *Jeongdaeeop*, for example have *bak* in the middle of a stanza. Also, the number of strikes has little to do with the text structure, its number having decreased in general. This can be summarized as follows.

The rhythm resulting from text construction has changed rather irregularly. Text rhythm refers to the fact that text is placed in regular and repeated fashion in Jeongganbo, producing a musical rhythm, although it lacks any pitch change. The text rhythm found in *Sejo sillok* depends on the text form of 3 *eon* (syllables), 4 *eon*, 5 *eon*, and is also categorized into the three musical styles, beginning in the first, second, and third *daegang*.

Among the styles beginning in the third *daegang*, the text–influenced rhythm is found in 10 movements, including the three pieces of "Huimun" in Yeongsin, Jeonpye, and Inip, "Hyeonmi," "Daeyu," "Somu," "Takjeong," "Sinjeong," "Suneung," and "Jeongse." Texts in this style occur in three types : 1 *gu* 5 *eon* (five syllables in a line), 1 *gu* 4 *eon* (four syllables in a line), and 1 *gu* 3 *eon* (three syllables in a line), and the general rule is that eight *jeonggan* make up one basic unit.

Movements with text rhythm beginning in the second *daegang* are "Yonggwang" and "Hyeokjeong." The texts in this style consist of 1 *gu* 4 *eon*, and the text rhythm for this is 5 · 5 · 3 · 3/2 · 3 · 5 · 3/5 · 3 · 5 · 6 in its *jeonggan* unit. Text rhythm for music beginning in the second *daegang* is characteristically shorter in cycle than that for music beginning in the third *daegang*.

Examples of the musical style beginning in the first *daegang* are the twelve movements, "Punganjiak," "Gimyeong," "Hyeongga," "Jimnyeong," "Yunghwa," "Jeongmyeong," "Yeokseong," "Dokgyeong," "Seonwi," "Bunung," "Chongyu," and "Yeonggwan," all having 1 *gu* 4 *eon*. Text rhythmic patterns for music beginning in the first *daegang* come in three types : a 16 · 16 · 16 · 16 *jeonggan* unit, a 5 · 3 · 5 · 3 *jeonggan* unit, and an 8 · 8 · 8 · 8 *jeonggan* unit. Text rhythm for this style commonly uses the 5 · 3 · 5 · 3 *jeonggan* unit, with the 16 · 16 · 16 · 16 *jeonggan* unit used slightly less often. The 8 · 8 · 8 · 8 *jeonggan* unit is found only in "Jeongmyeong."

Therefore, the lyrics for *Jongmyo jeryeak* originally contained text–rhythmic structures resulting from the number of syllables in each stanza, which is rarely seen in *Jongmyo jeryeak* today.

The melodic rhythm of *Jongmyo jeryeak* occurred in various types according to the number of *jeonggan* : 16 *jeonggan*, 8 *jeonggan*, or 5 *jeonggan*. However, such melodic rhythm was lost by the time of the publication of *Akjangyoram*, with each note having become one or two beats.

(3) Intertones

Present–day melodies on *piri*, *daegeum*, and *haegeum* in *Jongmyo jeryeak* are much more complicated than those in their original forms. Added melodies are categorized as embellishment, added melodies, and intertones. Embellishment refers to the addition of grace notes on the original note. For example, Hwang (C) is embellished as Nam Hwang (A'-C), with Nam (A') acting as a grace note for Hwang (C). Added melodies indicate that a new melody appears in addition to the original melody. For example, if we look at the *akjang* text "*mak bul sol jong*" in "Yunghwa" in *Botaepyeong*, the original Im (G) for "*sol*" is changed to Im Nam Hwang Tae Hwang (林南潢汰潢, G-A-c-d-c), extending the melody as a result. Intertones occur when the original note is turned into multiple notes; the original note is followed by a note a major 2nd, minor 3rd, perfect 4th, or perfect 5th higher, which then returns to the original note.

In *Botaepyeong*, intertones are most expressively used in Hwang, Jung, Im, Nam, Hwang, Tae, and Jung (黃仲林南潢汰仲, C-F-G-A-c-d-F), while in *Jeongdaeeop*, they appear in Hwang, Hyeop, Jung, Im, Mu, Hwang, Hyeop, and Jung (黃夾仲林無潢浹仲, C-Eb-F-G-A-c-eb-F).

Akjang : A Literature Genre and Song Type

Akjang : A Literature Genre and Song Type

Akjang is both a type of literature and vocal music created for rituals and banquets held in the court. It praises past kings or present rulers, by which to underscore the legitimacy of the dynasty. *Akjang* is only one section of *Jongmyo jeryeak*, but since it directly praises the royal ancestors, it was considered to be the most important element of the ritual.

Akjang in *Botaepyeong* and *Jeongdaeeop* extols the virtues of the ancestors who founded the country. *Botaepyeong* explains that spirits of the forefathers help to maintain peace among the people, develop a good culture, and keep the country safe from enemies. *Jeongdaeeop* recounts how ancestors have contributed in dealing with foreign powers, including China, the Red turban Bandits, and Japan, as well as with Goryeo officials who opposed the establishment of the Joseon Dynasty. In *aak* performance, *akjang* was typically sung by the *deungga* ensemble during Jeonpye, Choheon, and Cheolbyeondu, but as *Botaepyeong* and *Jeongdaeeop* came to be included in *Jongmyo jeryeak*, it was sung for all sections, by both the *deungga* ensemble and the *heonga* ensemble. The person who actually sings *akjang* was called the *dochang*.

During Japanese occupation, the *akjang* lyrics were distorted, and used to denigrate the Joseon court and conceal the Japanese invasion of Daema Island [Tsushima Island], but today, the original lyrics have been revived.

1. Song Texts and Background of *Akjang*

1) Yeongsin (迎神) – "Huimun" (熙文)

Your great virtue cultivated from generation to
generation gave birth to your descendants,
Ah, ah! We can clearly imagine the sight and sound!
We offer our sacrificial rite in a dignified manner,
Please grant us peace and our wishes.

2) Jeonpye (奠幣) – "Huimun"

Although it is of no value, your modesty would accept this
small offering,
We offer you this basket with our obeisance.

Please accept our offering with pleasure,
We pay you our sincere homage.

3) Jinchan (進饌) – "Punganjiak" (豊安之樂)

I diligently prepare rice,
Place it in the sacred bowl.
I offer you food in the sacrificial utensil and,
Play music in proper order.
Since I burn incense and offer this wine,
Please, grant us your help.

4) Choheon (初獻) – *Botaepyeong* (保太平)

(1) "Huimun"

As you, holy ancestors, have opened shining luck,
The bright and prosperous civil governing has been disclosed.
To praise what is grand and fair,
We sing this song.

"Huimun" means to praise literate rule. This song is called "Iniphuimun," since it is sung when the offering official enters the chamber.

(2) "Gimyeong" (基命)

Oh, our great Mokjo,
He floated on the ocean and moved to Gyeongwon.
More and more people came to him,
Our great father founded an eternal kingdom.

"Gimyeong" deals with how Mokjo moved from Jeonju via Samcheok to Odong to found the dynasty. It appears in the third chapter of *Yongbieocheonga* (龍飛御天歌, Songs of the Dragons Flying to Heaven) and is identical to "Gyeu," the first section of the first chapter of *Botaepyeong* during King Sejong's period.

Mokjo first lived in Jeonju, but a *sanseong byeolgam* (山城別監, an official charged with protecting a mountain fortress during Goryeo period) stole his beloved *gisaeng* (female entertainer). This resulted in a feud with the official, who then attempted to kill Mokjo. Knowing this, Mokjo moved to Samcheok, Gangwon Province, and 170 households followed him. After they settled in Samcheok, his rival, the *sanseong byeolgam,* came to Anryeomsa, Samcheok as his post. When Mokjo learned this, he again moved with his family across the ocean to reach Deogwonbu, Hamgil Province. The 170 families from Jeonju moved along with him. Later, he submitted himself to the Chinese Yuan Dynasty and moved to Odong. When the Chinese emperor appointed him as a *darughachi* (a civil–military official in the Mongol empire) for 5,000 households, he was welcomed and praised by everyone in the province. This was the foundation of Joseon's royal family.[1)]

(3) "Gwiin" (歸仁)

How great is our lord!
You have prepared the land for your people.
You cared for this small plot of land,
Grant us your bright light.
Since you have such great virtue,
People follow you like a shadow.
Although so many people follow you,
You did not think of it as your personal benefit.
You did not think of it for your personal sake,
Knowing people return to men of great virtue.
As returning to a man of great virtue
The broad foundation is set.

This song deals with the story of Ikjo when he returned to Deogwonbu from Jeokdo and was greeted by a great number of people. This story appears in the fourth chapter of *Yongbieocheonga* and is the same as that of "Uiin" in the first section of the second chapter of *Botaepyeong* during King Sejong's period.

1) Kim Seong-chil, 1985. "Yongbieocheonga," *Sejong* (Seoul : Donghwa chulpansa); Yun Ho-jin, 2006. *Yeokjuagwongosa* (Seoul : Gungnipgugagwon); *Sejong sillok* (*The Annals of King Sejong*) Vol. 138.28b; *Daeakhubo* Vol 2.13a (Seoul : Gungnipgugagwon).

Ikjo made a great name for himself while living in Odong, and a great number of people followed him. This caused other lords to envy him, and plot to kill Ikjo. Ikjo fled them and lived in a cave in Jeokdo. When people learned that he had moved there, they all followed him. Later, Ikjo returned to Deogwonbu and his followers at Gyeongheung were great in number.[2)]

(4) "Hyeongga" (亨嘉)

Oh! Great is your name, Ikjo!
He obeyed the king out of great respect.
Our sacred Dojo followed his will,
Their great love and reliance for each other increased every day,
By the heaven's command they came to rule our land.

"Hyeongga" deals with Ikjo and Dojo, whose family faithfully served the king of Goryeo, earning the full trust of the king. It is analogous to "Hyeonggwang," the first section of the third chapter of *Botaepyeong* during King Sejong's time.

(5) "Jimnyeong" (輯寧)

Ssangseong is so far away,
People say it is the place in heaven.
Since the official neglected his duty,

2) Kim Seong–chil, *ibid*.; Yun Ho–jin, *ibid*.; *Daeakhubo* Vol 2.15b.

The people suffer.

As our sacred Hwanjo took care of them,

The wandering people finally returned home.

He received a calling from the heaven,

And established a blissful kingdom.

"Jimnyeong" tells the story of Hwanjo who helped the people of Ssangseong regain their occupations. It appears in the twenty–fourth chapter of *Yongbieocheonga* and is analogous to "Bodae" of *Botaepyeong* in King Sejong's time.

Ssangseong is located in the outer frontier. Using the empress' power, the family and relatives of Gihwanghu (奇皇后, Empress Gi (Ki), originally from Goryeo, who became an empress of Huizing (1320–1370) in the Chinese Yuan Dynasty) became tyrants. Gi Cheol, the queen's brother, plotted revolt by making alliance with the rebels of Ssangseong. The king therefore ordered Hwanjo to rule the people there, after which they all came to live and work in peace. Later, when Hwanjo entered the court, the king greeted him with the words, "Is it not difficult to rule peacefully such wild and obstinate people?"[3)]

(6) "Yunghwa" (隆化)

Oh! How great and sacred is our great king, Taejo!

How great is your virtue!

3) Kim Seong–chil, *ibid.*; Yun Ho–jin, *ibid.*; *Daeakhubo* Vol 2.18a; *Sejong sillok* Vol. 138.31b.

For you have ruled with your grace and won their hearts with your
sense of justice,
Everyone who is edified by your godly nature is satisfied.
From barbarians from the faraway islands
To savages of the mountains,
You embrace them all,
So that there is no one not following you.
Sailing on the sea, or climbing a ladder,
People would follow my[Taejo] name.
Oh, how brilliant is your spirit!
You make peace near and tranquilize afar.

"Yunghwa" describes how King Taejo, to whom barbarians and savages paid homage, made people all over the land live in peace with his austerity and virtue. It appears in the ninth chapter of *Yongbieocheonga* and is analogous to "Yunghwa" of *Botaepyeong* in King Sejong's period.

After King Taejo received the calling, his influence reached to faraway barbarians, who changed their attitude, and permitted merchants to resume their trade. Chiefs of savage tribes all surrendered. He expanded his land east and west, and met with millions of followers.

(7) "Hyeonmi" (顯美)

Oh! Our great King Taejong,
Recovered peace and saved our country!
Although people paid high tribute to his charitable deeds and had great confidence in him,
He yielded the throne graciously, showing his true virtue.

"Hyeonmi" deals with the story of King Taejong, who, after suppressing Jeong Do–jeon's rebellion, was asked to become the next heir to the throne. Taejong declined the offer and yielded this honor to Gongjeongwang (King Jeongjong, r. 1398–1400). Jeongjong replied, "From the founding of this country to present case, Taejong's role was indispensible. I cannot take the honor," but Taejong would not accept.[4)] This also appears in the ninety–ninth chapter of Yongbieocheonga, and was recorded in "Seunggang" of *Botaepyeong* during Sejong's reign.

(8) "Yonggwang–Jeongmyeong" (龍光貞明)

When the Emperor of China showed his anger,
This caused fear and worry in all people.
King Taejong then entered the court to speak to the Emperor,
A proof of his patriotism.
He was greeted by the Emperor,

4) Kim Seong–chil, *ibid.*; Yun Ho–jin, *ibid.*; *Daeakhubo* Vol 2.21a; *Sejong sillok* Vol. 138.33a.

His glory is great!
Benevolent Queen Wongyeong is
A match made in heaven.
Her deeds in tranquilizing the country,
Helping our king are beautiful indeed.
How fair, how bright and glorious!
She led our people to a blissful state.

"Yonggwang" explains that King Taejong, during a time of political turmoil, went to China to face the emperor and was warmly greeted. It appears in the ninety-fourth chapter of *Yongbieocheonga* and is analogous to "Changhwi" of *Botaepyeong* during Sejong's period.

During King Taejo's reign, the Chinese emperor became furious and sent a letter of complaint, condemning the fact that Joseon had seduced a Chinese general with silk and gold and let barbarians cross the Amnok River. Jeong Do-jeon wrote a response to this, but made the emperor even angrier with his haughty sentences, and finally, the emperor refused to accept Joseon ambassadors five times. King Taejo decided that Taejong was the only one who could deal with the emperor and sent him instead. Taejong arrived in Gyeongsa and met the emperor three times to explain the whole thing. The emperor appreciated his sincere attempts and told his officials to grant him a safe return home.[5)]

5) Kim Seong-chil, *ibid.*; Yun Ho-jin, *ibid.*; *Daeakhubo* Vol 2.24a; *Sejong sillok* Vol. 138.35a.

"Jeongmyeong" recounts the story of how Queen Wongyeong's wisdom helped solve the case of Jeong Do–jeon's rebellion. It appeared in the 109th chapter of *Yongbieocheonga* and is identical to "Jeongmyeong" of *Botaepyeong* during King Sejong's time. When Jeong's revolt broke out, Queen Wongyeong, plotting with her brother general, succeeded in securing arms and soldiers, saying to the rebels that they were for her own private protection. Later, when Taejong succeeded the throne and made her queen, he announced, "she has helped greatly in pacifying our country with her wit and wisdom. Her contribution to my success is great indeed."[6)]

(9) "Junggwang" (重光)

Oh, our great King Seonjo,
Shined with such great virtue!
He set everything right in China,
Saved our kingdom.
He rid the country of barbarians with his righteousness,
Defined our national boundaries.
With heavenly bliss we have entered into a new period,
Shiny and eternally promising!

"Junggwang" is a story of King Seonjo which was amended in 1626 (the fourth year of King Injo). King Seonjo contributed in vindicating ancestors

6) Kim Seong-chil, ibid.; Yun Ho-jin, ibid.; Daeakhubo,ibid.; Sejong sillok , ibid.

and raising the country's name. He also defeated the Japanese army in great number, a great and praiseworthy deed.[7)]

(10) "Daeyu" (大猷)

Sacred ancestors shone their name repeatedly and
Made people live in peace with their civil ruling.
Having already established law and institutions,
Their wisdom shines great.

"Daeyu" explains that all the kings have been great with their civil virtue and thus their rules ensure a peaceful and just kingdom. It is the same as "Daedong" of *Botaepyeong* from King Sejong's period.[8)]

(11) "Yeokseong" (繹成)

What the ancestors have pursued with great virtue
Are the achievements we are following.
Our kingdom prospers
In your sense of decorum and music.
With *yak* held in left hand and *jeok* in the right,
They have already established it all.
Revealing the splendid triumphs of the ancestors,

7) Yun Ho-jin, *ibid.*; *Daeakhubo* Vol 2.26b.

8) *Daeakhubo* Vol 2.28ab; *Sejong sillok* Vol. 138.36b.

Which are so beautiful and wonderful.

"Yeokseong" is played when the officiant is led outside.

5) Aheon (亞獻) · Jongheon (終獻) – *Jeongdaeeop* (定大業)

(1) "Somu" (昭武)

Heaven has helped our glorious armies,
Praised their sacred valor.
In praise of such mighty deeds,
We sing and dance.

"Somu" is played when the officiant is assisted inside.

(2) "Dokgyeong" (篤慶)

Oh! Our great and holy Mokjo,
Raised his flag up north.
In confirming this propitious event,
Our ancestors have created a new dynasty.

"Dokgyeong" describes how Mokjo, when he lived in Odong, became head of five thousand families, which became the foundation of a new kingdom. It appears in the third chapter of *Yongbieocheonga* and is

"Dokgyeong" of *Botaepyeong* during King Sejong's reign.[9)]

(3) "Takjeong" (濯征)

Those obstinate barbarians are
Hiding in Ssangseong.
Our great Hwanjo
Has cleared them all.
He defeated those sly wild creatures,
Made a land for our people.

"Takjeong" is a story about Hwanjo which appears in the twenty-fourth chapter of *Yongbieocheonga*.

Daesado Gi Cheol, the brother of Empress Gi, secretly gathered people in Ssangseong, and created a rebellious party to aid revolt. The king communicated what was revealed of the plan to Hwanjo and ordered him to restore Ssangseong. Hwanjo made an attack on the headquarters in Ssangseong with Yu In–u and Kim Won–bong, and was victorious. Jo So–saeng and Tak Do-gyeong, who led the revolt, fled into the night, deserting their own families. Hwanjo and his men then consulted maps to restore other castles.[10)]

9) Kim Seong–chil, *ibid.*; Yun Ho–jin, *ibid.*; *Daeakhubo* Vol 2.35a.

10) Kim Seong–chil, *ibid.*; Yun Ho–jin, *ibid.*; *Daeakhubo* Vol 2.38a; *Sejong sillok* Vol. 138.5b.

(4) "Seonwi" (宣威)

Ah! As Goryeo was not governed properly
Received attacks from all quarters.
Island barbarians came biting,
Thieves of Nahachu sneered.
Red Turban Bandits went wild,
Remnants of the Yuan soldiers were violent.
Wicked Buddhist monks would have their ways,
Savage chiefs are running wild.
Oh, our great Taejo
Shone with his sacred military deeds.
He revealed heaven's power,
How glorious and marvelous he was!

"Seonwi" is about the time when Taejo defeated the Japanese repeatedly, drove away Nahachu (a general of the Yuan Dynasty), suppressed the Red Turban Bandits, restored Olla, conquered Dongnyeong, repelled Prince Deokheung, and destroyed Hobaldo(a chief of the Jurchens) to restore peace in the country. It appears in the fiftieth chapter of *Yongbieocheonga* and is "Hyeokjeong" of *Jeongdaeeop* during King Sejong's reign.

In 1361 (the tenth year of King Gongmin's reign), the Red Turban Bandits attacked Seoul and conquered the country. Taejo was ordered to assist the prime minister to defeat the enemy and restore the city. Also, when Nahachu invaded the northeastern territory and arrived in Goju, Hamgyeong

Province, Taejo received orders to go there and drive them all out. In 1363 (the twelfth year of King Gongmin's reign), when Prince Deokheung, a child of a concubine, made a revolt against the king of Goryeo, Taejo, with a small number of soldiers, went and defeated him. In 1377 (the third year of King U), when the Japanese invaded, Taejo, in the frontier, killed most of them with his own hands. Also in 1380 (the sixth year of King U) the Japanese invaded three southern provinces and so the king appointed Taejo to take patrol duty in provinces of Yanggwang, Jeolla, and Gyeongsang to defeat them. Taejo went out with his men and bravely defeated them all.[11)]

(5) "Sinjeong" (神定)

He became furious to our enemy,
Fought like a tiger or a puma.
As he was so valorous,
It looked like he was flying.
He moved gods in heaven
With his righteous heart.
As grass is cut down with an ax,
They collapsed instantly.
Destroyed like split bamboo,
Who could withstand such a formidable attack?
His military deeds were so great,

11) Kim Seong-chil, *ibid.*; Yun Ho-jin, *ibid.*; *Daeakhubo* Vol 2.40b; *Sejong sillok* Vol. 138.8b and Vol. 139.8a.

It is work done by spirits.

"Sinjeong" generally describes Taejo's valor as a warrior and his moral virtue.[12)]

(6) "Bunung" (奮雄)

I am strong and brave,
Like thunder and lightning.
Nothing is too strong for me,
No task is too difficult for me to handle.
I capture enemy by dozens,
Attain their ears as war trophies.
With one shake of my sacred spear,
Wicked spirits are all gone.
No one shall offend nor bother us,
What a blessing to our country!

"Bunung" is general description of Taejo defeating his enemies.[13)]

(7) "Suneung" (順應)

The king of Goryeo did not listen to words of wisdom,

12) Kim Seong–chil, *ibid.*; Yun Ho–jin, *ibid.*; *Daeakhubo* Vol 2.48b; *Sejong sillok* Vol. 138.16a.

13) Kim Seong–chil, *ibid.*; Yun Ho–jin, *ibid.*; *Daeakhubo* Vol 2.53a; *Sejong sillok* Vol. 139.13a.

So I must rise in revolt.
God will judge our fortune,
As we turn back our soldiers,
Heaven and the people are on our side.

"Suneung" is a story of Taejo and appears in the ninth chapter of *Yongbieocheonga*.

King U of Goryeo said he wanted to hunt at Baeksajeong, making an excuse to carry out military actions, and ordered his men to attack Yodong, to which Taejo, Yi Seong–gye, objected. But the army was stationed across the Amnok River at Wihwa Island. Thinking that crossing the border would do harm to his people, Yi Seong–gye convinced his men to turn back. Although many days of rain had not flooded the island, when they reached the shore, there was a big flood. People thought this very strange.[14)]

(8) "Chongsu" (寵綏)

He raised his righteous flag and turned back,
Heaven helped him greatly.
Heaven trembles deeming it noble,
The people were mad with joy.
Since he was there to make peace in the world,
Everyone greeted him with a new jar of sauce.

14) Kim Seong–chil, *ibid*.; Yun Ho–jin, *ibid*.; Daeakhubo Vol 2.54b; Sejong sillok Vol. 139.15b.

Since he has chased away what is bad and ugly

Our kingdom will last as long as the clear eastern ocean.

"Chongsu" deals with Taejo's withdrawal of army troops at Wihwa Island, and appears in the ninth chapter of *Yongbieocheonga*. Before the withdrawal, a song circulated thus : "light is seen outside Seogyeong Castle and smoke is rising from Anju Castle. Hope the lord roaming within saves us all." Another song went, "Mokja (木子) will win this country." These songs were sung when the withdrawing army passed through. When the army passed through Seogyeong and reached Gyeongseong, former servants of King U cheered with glee. When Yi Seong–gye entered Sungin Gate, men and women rushed towards his men with soy sauce. Women and children hurried to make a way and elders shouted with glee from high towers. The next day, Uwang went to Ganghwa.[15)]

(9) "Jeongse" (靖世)

The lonely vassal,

Has caused disaster.

Our ancestors,

Have shed light in the world.

His formidable wisdom defeated the enemies,

Brought peace to the land.

15) Kim Seong–chil, *ibid.*; Yun Ho–jin, *ibid.*; *Daeakhubo* Vol 2.58b; *Sejong sillok* Vol. 139.18a.

"Jeongse" is a story of Taejong and appears in chapter 109 of *Yongbieocheonga*. Jeong Do–jeon(1342–1398) and Nam Eun(1354–1398) conspired to take over the throne, promoted a young prince and attempted to kill the rest. Taejo became ill and Jeong Do–jeon, with the intention of changing the king, invited the princes into court to get rid of them. Foreseeing all this, Queen Wongyeong secured armed men in secret in preparation. When the event broke, Taejong came out from Yeongchu Gate and, aided only by the queen's men, defeated Jeong Do–jeon and his followers.[16)]

(10) "Hyeokjeong" (赫整)

Insular barbarians, with little reason,
Would invade our territory.
Our furious king
Dispatched his army.
Countless sailboats
Went across the ocean as if flying.
They destroyed the enemies and killed them all.
It was like plucking feathers from a wild goose
Burning them in a blazing fire.
The big wave ceased,
Our country regained peace.

16) Kim Seong–chil, *ibid.*; Yun Ho–jin, *ibid.*; *Daeakhubo* Vol 2.60a; *Sejong sillok* Vol. 139.20.

"Hyeokjeong" is a story of King Taejong. According to *Akwongosa*(樂院故事), "In 1419 (the first year of King Sejong's reign), the Japanese invaded Daema Island in July. The king appointed generals with orders, but asked an oarsman to attack the island." Although it is dated as being in Sejong's time, it was King Taejong who gave this order.[17)]

(11) "Yeonggwan" (永觀)

Oh, our great ancestor,
Showed glorious military deeds.
All their achievements and success,
How could words describe?
Our dance is formed in order,
The exit and ending are well–mannered.
It shows dignified and natural grace that
Describe the eternal glory of our country.
This movement is played when the officiant is led outside.

6) Cheolbyeondu (徹籩豆) – "Onganjiak" (雍安之樂)

Our ritual utensils are full to the rim,
Overflowing *dugi* (豆器) and *byeongi* (籩器).
As the sacrificial offering is so fragrant,

17) Kim Seong–chil, *ibid.*; Yun Ho–jin, *ibid.*; *Daeakhubo* Vol 2.62a; *Sejong sillok* Vol. 139.23a.

Our ancestors have arrived for sure.

Concluding the sacrificial offering that we have made,

Report that the meal has come to a close.

7) Songsin (送神) – "Heunganjiak" (興安之樂)

As the sacrificial ritual has properly ended

The spirits are satisfied and delighted.

On leaving us,

They turn back to take a look.

Like a banner of rainbow

They shall rise over the clouds.

2 · Musical Characteristics of *Akjang*

Throughout history, *akjang* has been transmitted orally by musicians; the *akjang* existing at present was recorded by Yi Su–gyeong (1882–1955). Since *Sejo sillok*, all *Jongmyo jeryeak* music records did not include separate scores for *akjang*, and the first independently–written record of *akjang* was *Jurye juaguiju* (周禮奏樂儀註, *Rites of Zhou*) made at the time of Yiwangjik aakbu. This is more of a transitional version to our present Jeongganbo notation, but the melody contained there is not much different from that used today.

In terms of mode for *akjang*, *Botaepyeong* is in *pyeongjo*, consisting of Hwang·Tae·Jung·Im and Nam (C–D–F–G–A) while *Jeongdaeeop* uses the mode Mu·Hyeop·Jung and Im ($B^{b'}$–E^{b}–F–G), (perfect 4th– major 2nd– major 2nd), with Hwang (C) changed to Mu ($B^{b'}$) and Im (G) to Jung (F). In other words, the pitch range is expanded a major 2nd, and intervals of the perfect 4th and major 2nd are maintained.

There is also a special principle for pronunciation when singing *akjang*. Some vowels are pronounced in an extended version. For example, *gi* is sung *geu*–i, and *bi*, as *bu*–i. *Ui* is pronounced *eu–i*, *oe* as *o–i*, *ae* as *a–i*, and *wi* as *u–i*. Also the four voiced sounds, "ㅇ," "ㄴ," "ㄹ," and "ㅁ" are sounded beginning with vowel sounds first combined with added voiced consonants and proceeding with a nasal sound at the next sound.

Another feature of *akjang* is *iptaryeong*, that is, singing of the non–lexical vowel, "*ae*." In general, *iptaryeong* is interposed between stanzas with any non–lexical syllables. But in *Jongmyo jeryeak*, this is inserted between words with the vowel. Since it is a meaningless syllable, it is similar to *iptaryeong*.

Movements that do not include singing of the "*ae*" syllable are "Jimnyeong," "Junggwang," "Yeokseong," "Gwiin," "Hyeongga," "Yunghwa," and "Yonggwang–Jeongmyeong" in *Botaepyeong*; and "Bunung," "Hyeokjeong," "Yeonggwan," and "Chongsu" in *Jeongdaeeop*. Except for "Yonggwang," these are all pieces that begin in the first *daegang*. Therefore, we can assume that pieces beginning in the second or third *daegang* have relatively more "*ae*" singing in their music.

Ilmu : The Dance in the Royal Ancestral Ritual

Ilmu : The Dance in the Royal Ancestral Ritual

1 . Theoretical Background of *Ilmu*

According to the *Akgi* (樂記, Record of Music) section of *Yegi*, the representative ancient source on music, "music springs from the human heart but it is the outer materials which move one's heart. Humans act on material to produce sound (*seong*, 聲) and different sounds interact, change, and structure to become notes (*eum*, 音). When melody is played with instruments to reach the level of *gancheok–umo* (干戚羽旄), this becomes music (*ak*, 樂)." *Gancheok* here refers to the dance implements used in *mumu* (武舞, military dance), while *umo* designates those used in *munmu* (文舞, civil dance). Therefore, *gancheok–umo* refers to dance itself. If we read the *Akgi* section of *Yegi* informed by such knowledge, it seems that music is played with musical instruments but must also have dance to accompany it, in order to truly become music. In other words, one must have sound, music, and dance altogether in order to have a complete *ak*–defined in the *Akgi* as an inseparable coupling of music and sound.

In a sense, dance itself is already a ritual performance. The *Chungwan* (春官, Rites Officials) section of *Jurye* (周禮, the State System of the Zhou Dynasty) states that "ritual is defined as dance with *uyak* (羽籥)." That is, ritual is conducted with *uyak* dance. This leads us to believe that a ritual without dance was unthinkable, and this is, in fact, the point that *Akgi* was trying to make. As the sentence, "When melody is played with instruments to reach the level of *gancheok–umo,* this becomes music," implies, *gancheok–umo* is the primary agent, whereas the melody and instruments embellish it. Music is used to adorn dance. However, in general, people tend to consider dance as subordinate to music.

The *So* (疏) passage in the *Chungwan* section of *Jurye* directs "Enhance the atmosphere with dance of *uyak* and harmonize it with musical phrases so as to support each in keeping the order." Here, it is emphasized that *uyak* dance should create balance and harmonize with music. In other words, *eum, ak*, and *mu* are three basic and inseparable elements. Ancient Koreans always included dance in their rituals–already a combination of *eum*, *ak*, and *mu*. Thus, *yeak* (禮樂, formal music) should always include the three basic elements of *eum* and *ak*, as well as *mu*.

Jeryeak (祭禮樂, sacrificial ritual music) consisted of *ak*(instrumental music), *ga* (the singing of *akjang*), and *mu* (dancing with *gancheok–umo*). *Ilmu* refers to court ritual dance, in which the dancers are positioned in lines, as "*il*" (佾) refers to "line."

This tradition of dancing in line is one of the major features of *aak*. *Aak* originated from ancient Chinese tradition, dating all the way back to the Chinese Zhou Dynasty. Dance performed as *aak* in the Zhou Dynasty was divided into *akmu* (樂舞), *daemu* (大舞), and *mu* (舞). *Akmu* refers to six kinds of music that deal with the six generations of ancient Chinese emperors or kings : the music of Hwangje (黃帝) is called *unmun* (雲門); the music of Yoje (堯帝) is called *hamji* (咸池); the music of Sunje (舜帝) is called *daeso* (大韶); the music of Uwang (禹王) is called *daeha* (大夏); the music of Tangwang (湯王) of the Shang Dynasty is called *daeho* (大濩); and the music of Muwang (武王) of the Zhou Dynasty is called *daemu* (大武). *Daemu* (大舞), on the other hand, refers to *unmunmu* (雲門舞), *daegwonmu* (大卷舞), daejangmu (大章舞), daehammu (大咸舞), *daegyeongmu* (大磬舞), and *daehamu* (大夏舞). Finally, *mu* (舞) includes *daehomu* (大護舞), *daemumu* (大武舞), *sangmu* (象舞), and *jakmu* (勺舞). In addition, there are also little dances, such as *bulmu* (帗舞), *umu* (羽舞), *hwangmu* (皇舞), momu (旄舞), *ganmu* (干舞), *inmu* (人舞), and *yamu* (野舞).[1] The *ilmu* performed in Korea would be categorized as a type of *akmu*.

The number of lines of dancers differs according to the status of the rite's subject. According to the *Eungongonyeonjo* (隱公五年條) section of *Chunchujwajeon* (春秋左傳, *Spring Autumn Left Annals*), from around the time of Eungong (Duke Yin) of the Lu (魯) State, the particular number of dancers

1) Jinyang, *Akseo* Vol. 165, p.168.

was designated as *parilmu* for an emperor, *yugilmu* for a feudal lord, *sailmu* for a noble lord, and for a scholar.

There are two theories that have survived over the years regarding the specific number of dancers in each category. One is from Duye (杜預) of the Chinese Jin Dynasty, and the other is from Bokgeon (服虔) of the Later Han Dynasty. The former has it that each file of dancers standing in a square should contain the same number of people. Thus, *parilmu* should contain sixty–four dancers in eight lines; *yugilmu*, thirty–six dancers in six lines; *sailmu*, sixteen dancers in four lines; and *iilmu*, four dancers in two lines. On the other hand, Bokgeon's theory holds that the first line of eight dancers should be fixed for all social statuses, and that, as the status rises, the rectangle of dancers would deepen and become more and more square. Thus, *parilmu* is danced with 64 dancers in 8 lines, but *yugilmu* should be performed by forty–eight dancers in six files and eight lines; likewise, in *sailmu*, thirty–two dancers in eight files and four lines; and *iilmu*, sixteen dancers in eight files and two lines.

Ilmu was first imported during the eleventh year of King Yejong's reign in the Goryeo period. In 1116, Hwijong (徽宗, r. 1100–1125) of the Chinese Song Dynasty sent *daeseongaak* (大晟雅樂) with *aak* instruments, costumes, dance implements, and other tools for both the *deungga* and *heonga* ensembles. Along with these items, also imported were *yak*, *jeok*, *gan*, and *gwa*, which were all implements for *ilmu*, thirty–six pieces for each. The number of each dance implement leads us to believe that what was transmitted in this case was *yugilmu*. For *ilmu* in *aak*, there are *munmu* and *mumu*. *Munmu* is danced for Yeongsin–rye, Jeonpye–rye, and Choheon–rye, while *mumu* is used for Aheon–rye and Jongheon–rye. For *munmu*, the *yak* and *jeok* are used as dance implements, while for *mumu*, *gan* (干, shield) and *cheok* (戚, ax) are employed.

From the founding of the Joseon Dynasty in 1392 to the eighth year of King Taejong's reign (1408), all costumes, implements, and music used in *Jongmyo jeryeak* followed the traditions of the Chinese Song Dynasty. In the following year, *aak* came to be used not only for ancestral rituals but also in court meetings and banquets. Until then, *aak* was used in ritual, but *jeonak* was played for court meetings, and *hyangak* and *dangak* were played in alternation at banquets. In the ninth year of King Sejong's reign (1427), there arose a controversy about using *hyangak* for the ancestral ritual. King Sejong ordered that scholars, with Pak Yeon in charge, consult old theoretical sources–*Jurye*, *Tongjeon* (通典, *Encyclopedic History of Institutions*), *Akseo*(樂書, *Treatise on Music*), *Seokjeonakbo* (釋奠樂譜, *Confucius Shrine Ritual Notation*), *Uiryegyeongjeontonghae*,(儀禮經傳通解, *Explanation on the Book of the Code of Courtesy*) and *Yulryosinseo* (律呂新書, *New Treatise on the System of Pitches*)–to arrive at the eight tones and devise a new system for *aak* more similar to the Chinese original. Therefore, from King Sejong's time to the ninth year of Sejo(1463), this renewed *aak* was used for all court ceremonies including rituals, meetings, and banquets. *Ilmu* was either "Yeolmunjimu" (*munmu*) or "Somujimu" (*mumu*). The tradition of *munmu* and *mumu*, performed in all sorts of rituals and banquets at the time, is still found in present–day *Munmyo jeryeak* (文廟祭禮樂, Confucian shrine ritual music). The *ilmu* for present–day *Jongmyo jerye* is the *ilmu* of *Botaepyeong* and *Jeongdaeeop*, which was created during King Sejong's time, and has been danced since King Sejo's reign.

2. The Background for Creation

In the seventh year of his reign (1425), King Sejong returned from an ancestral offering and said to Heojo (許稠), the minister of interior, "We feel most comfortable with *hyangak*. However, we are playing *dangak* first, for Choheon–rye and Aheon–rye, and it is not until we get to Jongheon–rye that we get to listen to some *hyangak*. Therefore, I suggest that, for serving our ancestors, we play what they enjoyed the most during their lives." In his twelfth year (1430), King Sejong raised the issue once more, saying "*Aak* is not really our music, and it is best to play what we feel to be familiar in our ancestral rituals. Is it not odd to be listening to *aak* after death, when all our lives we have listened to *hyangak*?"

In King Sejong's thirty–first year (1449), *Jeongdaeeop* and *Botaepyeong* were composed, to be played during court meeting and banquets. These two pieces contained many notes borrowed from *gochwiak* and *hyangak*. *Jeongdaeeop* contains fifteen pieces and *Botaepyeong* has eleven pieces. It is said that King Sejong himself composed the music overnight, while pounding a stick on the ground, and his son Suyangdaegun (首陽大君, later, King Sejo) commended dozens of the court ladies to learn the music.

As was previously detailed in the "Adoption of *Botaepyeong* and *Jeongdaeeop* as *Jongmyo jeryeak*" section in chapter two of this book, King Sejo ordered Choe Hang to reorganize *Botaepyeong* and *Jeongdaeeop* as eleven pieces each, while leaving their lyrics and original feeling of grandeur intact. King Sejo also designated this music as *Jongmyo jeryeak*. *Botaepyeong* and *Jeongdaeeop* were also used for other occasions. *Jeongdaeeop* was used for *jinpungjeong* (進豊呈, large–scale court banquets for joyful occasions) while both *Jeongdaeeop* and *Botaepyeong* were played for *yangnoyeon*(養老宴, the feast for elderly people) when the king and queen gave a banquet in the court. The dance for *Botaepyeong* praises the civil virtue of kings, while that for *Jeongdaeeop* celebrates their military skill.

The dances were performed in the form of *yugilmu*, in commemoration of the art and military achievements of past kings of the Joseon Dynasty. On the founding of the Korean Empire, in order to pay homage to the new emperor, dance was performed as *parilmu*. However, this was downgraded to *yugilmu* once again during the Japanese occupation, and later returned to *parilmu* after liberation and the founding of the Republic of Korea.

3 . Transmission and Change of *Ilmu*

1) Number of Dancers and Attire

Gukjooryeui records that the dancers are situated north of the *heonga* ensemble, with six dancers in a line, holding *yak* in the left hand and *u* in the right, facing north. Two *duk* (纛, flags) should stand north of the dancers. It also states that "Musicians should all wear *jinhyeongwan* (進賢冠, formal hat for government officials), *namui* (藍衣, blue robe), *jeoksangjoyeon* (赤裳皂緣, red skirt biased with black cloth), *jeokmaldae* (赤抹帶, red belt), *baekpomal* (白布襪, white socks), and *opiri* (烏皮履, black leather shoes for musicians)."

According to *Akhakgwebeom*, *Botaepyeong* features, among its thirty–eight performers, thirty–six dancers and two flag holders. They all wear *jinhyeongwan*, *namjuui* (藍紬衣, blue robe), *jeoksangjoyeon*, *jeokmaldae*, *baekpomal*, and *opiri*, holding *yak* with the left hand and *jeok* in the right. It is written that *Botaepyeong* is danced for Yeongsin, Jeonpye, and Choheon. *Jeongdaeeop* is danced for Aheon and Jongheon. In dancing *Jeongdaeeop*, all seventy–one performers wear *pibyeon* (皮弁, hat made of deerskin) but otherwise their attire is the same as in *Botaepyeong* dance. Among the thirty–six dancers, those in the first two rows hold a sword, the middle two rows hold spears, and the last two rows, bows and arrows. The remaining thirty–five performers move holding ritual tools.

According to the *Jongmyosiyong botaepyeong jimudoseol* (宗廟時用保太平之舞圖說, Current Jongmyo Botaepyeong Dance Illustration) section of *Jongmyouigwe*, there are two flagbearers and thirty–six dancers in six lines, and all wear *jinhyeongwan*, *namjuui*, *jeoksangjoyeon*, *jeokmaldae*, *baekpomal*, and *opiri*, holding *yak* in the left hand and *jeok* in the right. Also, *Siyong jeongdaeeop jimudoseol* (時用定大業之舞圖說, Current Jeongdaeeop Dance Illustration) records that thirty–six dancers in six lines are featured, all wearing *pibyeon* and attired as civil dancers. The first two rows should hold swords, the next two rows, spears, and the final two rows, bows and arrows.

The *Gukjooryeui*, *Akhakgwebeom*, and *Jongmyouigwe* show that *yugilmu* features thirty–six dancers in six lines. *Botaepyeong* dancers wear *gwanbok* on their body and *jinhyeongwan* on their head, holding *yak* in the left hand and *jeok* in the right. Thirty–six dancers dance, while two flag holders stand in the front. *Jeongdaeeop* dancers wear *pibyongwan* and *gwanbok*, as well as *namui* or *namjuui*. The first two rows hold swords, the next two rows, spears, and the final two rows, bows and arrows. There are thirty–six dancers in total. In the east, south, and west, twenty–five *uijang* (儀仗, implement holders) hold *gak* (角, horn), *duk*, *go* (鼓, drum), *geum* (金, gong), and five–colored flags. Then, there are five *uijang* holding the flags of *jujakgi*, *cheongnyeonggi* (青龍旗, the flag of blue dragon), *hwangnyonggi*, *baekhogi*, and *hyeonmugi*, as well as another five for *na* (螺, conch shell), *daegak*, *daeduk* (大纛, large flag), *daego* (大鼓, large drum), and *daegeum* (large gong), for a total of seventy–one people.

In the *Siyong jeongdaeeopjimu* section of *Jongmyouigwe*, however, there is no record of *uijang*, only thirty–six *ilmu* dancers. This reflects the fact that the court could not afford to use music for their ancestral rituals following the double disasters of the Imjinwaeran and Byeongjahoran. In 1592 (the twenty–fifth year of King Seonjo's reign), when the Imjinwaeran broke out, both the main and sub–main shrines of *Jongmyo* were burned, and musicians died or gave up their professions. Also, musical instruments were broken or lost. Thus, ritual music became much reduced in scale compared to pre–war years. After Gwanghae–gun succeed the throne, he began to recover the ancestral ritual music, and, in 1610, *Akhakgwebeom* was reprinted, offering data on the past music and ritual system. In the fourth year of King Injo

(1626), *Botaepyeong* came to have an added movement, "Junggwang," after "Jeongmyeong."

However, these attempts to revive the ritual music soon met with another crisis. In 1636, the Byeongjahoran began, and many musicians and music students were either killed or captured as prisoners; no ancestral ritual was held for the next ten years. In 1765 (the forty–first year of King Yeongjo's

Figure 33. *Ilmu* arrangement for *Botaepyeong* and *Jeongdaeeop*

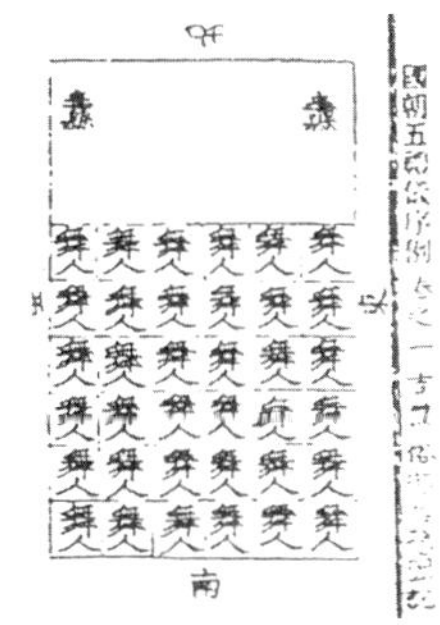

The *ilmu* arrangement for *Botaepyeong* in *Gukjooryeui*

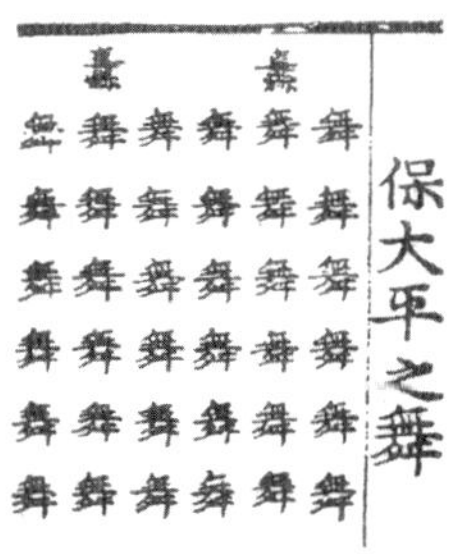

The *ilmu* arrangement for *Botaepyeong* in *Akhakgwebeom*

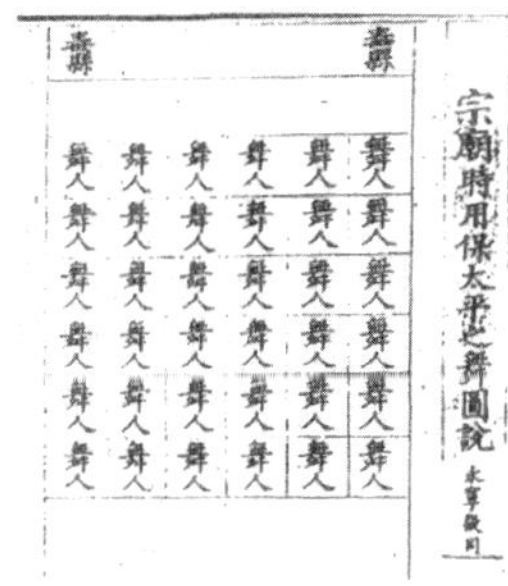

The *ilmu* arrangement for *Botaepyeong* in *Jongmyouigwe*

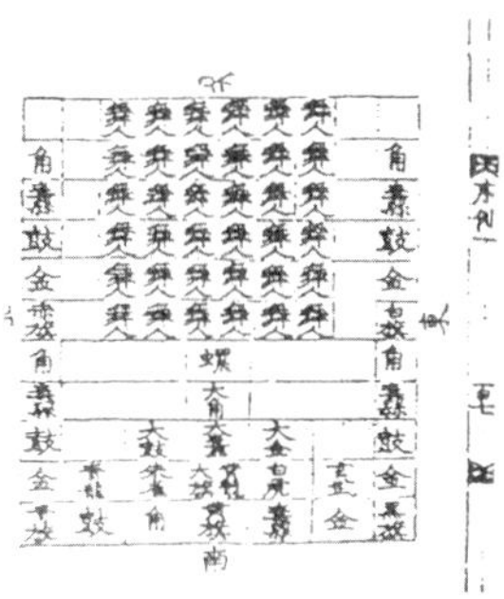

The *ilmu* arrangement for *Jeongdaeeop* in *Gukjooryeui*

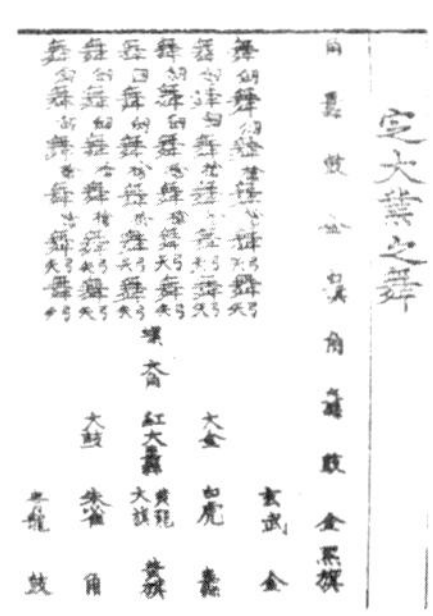

The *ilmu* arrangement for *Jeongdaeeop* in *Akhakgwebeom*

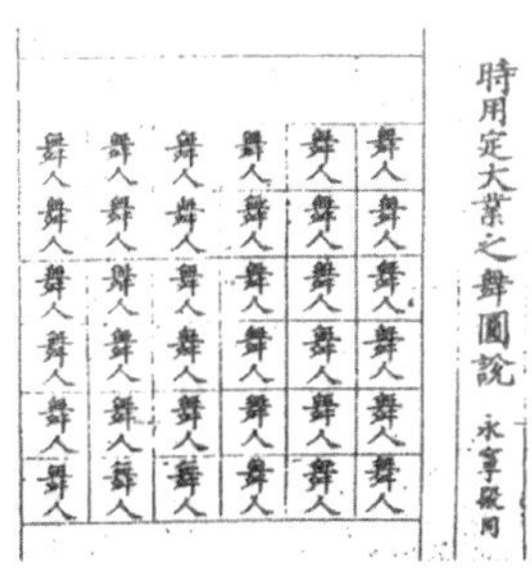

The *ilmu* arrangement for *Jeongdaeeop* in *Jongmyouigwe*

reign), "Yonggwang" and "Jeongmyeong" were combined into a single movement, so that *Botaepyeong* could maintain nine movements excluding the *inip* and *incul* sections.

In 1897, the thirty–fourth year of King Gojong's reign, the King declared the establishment of the Korean Empire, an independent state, and for the first time began using the indigenous era name of the state, Kwangmu (光武). This required elevation of all court ceremonies and rituals to the level of emperor. In particular, Wongudan (圓丘壇) was built and began presenting rituals to the heavens, a rite conducted only by an emperor. Therefore, in ancestral rituals and rituals offered to heaven, *ilmu* was danced in *parilmu* formation.

According to *Daehanyejeon* written in the year of *eulmi* (乙未; 1895), *munmu* required two flag bearers and sixty–four dancers in eight lines, holding *u* in the right hand and *yak* in the left hand. *Mumu* featured two *jeong* (旌, flag adorned with feathers) and also sixty–four dancers in eight lines, holding *gan* in the left hand and *cheok* in the right hand. All sixty–six performers wore *bokdu* (幞頭, square shaped–flat top hat for government officials) on their heads, and *hongpo* gowns and *namsadae* belts, as well as *baekpomal* and *opiri* on their feet.

Also, in *Jongmyo jerye*, the former level of lord was elevated to emperor and thus the formerly *yugilmu* event was now changed to *parilmu*, exclusively used for the emperor. According to *Daehanyejeon*, *Botaepyeong* should feature two *duk* and sixty–four dancers in eight lines, with *yak* in the left hand and *jeok* in the right hand. *Jeongdaeeop* required sixty–four dancers in eight lines, around which thirty–five performers with all kinds of ritual implements should stand in the east, west, and south. The attire of performers in *Jongmyo jerye* and for other civil court dances required *jinhyeongwan* with *namjuui, jeoksangjoyeon, jeokmaldae, baekpomal,* and *opiri*. Military attire required the addition of *pibyeon* but was otherwise the same as civil dancer attire, identical to that in *Gukjooryeui, Akhakgwebeom,* and *Jongmyouigwe.*

纛							纛										
舞人	舞人	舞人	舞人	舞人	舞人	舞人	舞人		舞人	舞人	舞人	舞人	舞人	舞人	舞人	舞人	
舞人	舞人	舞人	舞人	舞人	舞人	舞人	舞人		舞人	舞人	舞人	舞人	舞人	舞人	舞人	舞人	
舞人	舞人	舞人	舞人	舞人	舞人	舞人	舞人		舞人	舞人	舞人	舞人	舞人	舞人	舞人	舞人	
舞人	舞人	舞人	舞人	舞人	舞人	舞人	舞人	角	舞人	舞人	舞人	舞人	舞人	舞人	舞人	舞人	角
舞人	舞人	舞人	舞人	舞人	舞人	舞人	舞人	纛	舞人	舞人	舞人	舞人	舞人	舞人	舞人	舞人	纛
舞人	舞人	舞人	舞人	舞人	舞人	舞人	舞人	鼓	舞人	舞人	舞人	舞人	舞人	舞人	舞人	舞人	鼓
舞人	舞人	舞人	舞人	舞人	舞人	舞人	舞人	金	舞人	舞人	舞人	舞人	舞人	舞人	舞人	舞人	金
舞人	舞人	舞人	舞人	舞人	舞人	舞人	舞人	赤旗	舞人	舞人	舞人	舞人	舞人	舞人	舞人	舞人	白旗
								角				螺					角
								纛				大					纛
								鼓			大鼓	大纛		大金			鼓
								金	青龍		朱雀	大旗	黃旗	白虎		玄武	金
								青旗	鼓			黃旗		纛		金	黑旗

Figure 34. The *ilmu* arrangement for *Botaepyeong* (left) and *Jeongdaeeop* (right) in *Daehanyejeon*

However, records in the *Yitaewang gwangmuwonnyeon gaejeong munmumu dosik* (李太王光武元年改定文武舞圖式, Illustration of the Civil and Military Dance Modified in the First year of Gwangmu of Yi Great King) section of *Joseonakgaeyo* illustrate that *munmu* should comprise two *duk* and sixty–four dancers in eight lines; that *Botaepyeong* and *Jeongdaeeop* are the same in terms of dancers' attire; and that *Jeongdaeeop* should have sword, spear, and bow and arrow as dance implements. All sixty–six performers should wear *bokdu*, *hongjuui* (紅紬衣, red robe for musicians), and *namsadae*. In *mumu*, *jeong* is held instead of *duk*.

Correspondingly, instead of the red–dragon gown of kings, the emperor now wore a gold–dragon gown, and the dance was elevated from *yugilmu* to *parilmu*. The attire also changed, to *hongjuui* with *namsadae* and *bokdu*, for Wongudan. Also, in *Jongmyo jerye*, instead of the *namjuui* and *hongsadae* suitable for lords, dancers were now dressed in *hongjuui* with *namsadae* and *bokdu*.

In 1917, during the Japanese occupation period, *Joseonakgaeyo* makes mention of the *Botaehwa* (保太和) and *Hyangmannyeon* (享萬年) dances, which seem to be alternate names for the *Botaepyeong* and *Jeongdaeeop* dances, respectively. Dancers numbered thirty–six in six lines, and their attire consisted of *bokdu*, *hongjuui*, and *namsadae*. *Botaehwa* dance used *yak* and *jeok*, while *Hyangmannyeon* required sword, spear, bow, and arrow. In actuality, however, there was a serious shortage of dancers and thus the court only afforded a simplified substitute dance in Sambangbae (三方拜, lit., "three–

direction bowing") form with some borrowed dancers.

舞	舞	舞	舞	舞	舞	舞	舞	舞	舞	舞	舞
舞	舞	舞	舞	舞	舞	舞	舞	舞	舞	舞	舞
舞	舞	舞	舞	舞	舞	舞	舞	舞	舞	舞	舞
舞	舞	舞	舞	舞	舞	舞	舞	舞	舞	舞	舞
舞	舞	舞	舞	舞	舞	舞	舞	舞	舞	舞	舞
舞	舞	舞	舞	舞	舞	舞	舞	舞	舞	舞	舞

Figure 35. The *ilmu* arrangement for *Botaepyeong* (left) and *Jeongdaeeop* (right) in *Joseonakgaeyo*

Figure 36. Attire for *ilmu* dancers in *Akhakgwebeom*

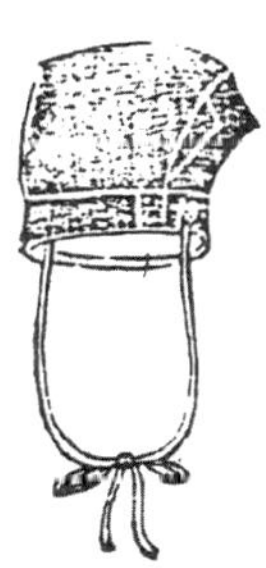

Jinhyeongwan

Pibyeon

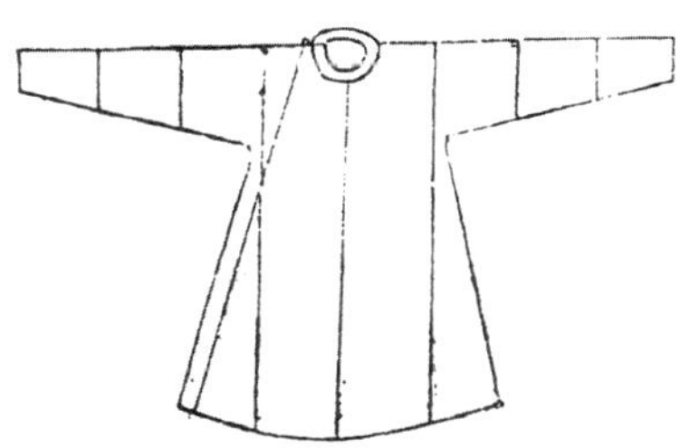

Namjuui

Jeokmaldae

Opiri

afforded a simplified substitute dance in Sambangbae (三方拜, lit., "three–direction bowing") form with some borrowed dancers.

After the Republic was established, *Jongmyo jeryeak* and *ilmu* were first performed in 1969. Everything was conducted on the scale of emperor, with *parilmu* and attire consisting of *hongjuui, namsadae, bokdu,* and *mokhwa* (木靴, half–boot–shaped shoes used in the middle and late periods of the Joseon Dynasty). Ritual implements comprised *yak* and *jeok* for *Botaepyeong,* and for *Jeongdaeeop,* the four front rows danced with swords and the back four rows with spears. The *hongjuui* kept at the royal shrine today is colored red–purple. Since 1997, the Preservation Committee of the Ancestral Shrine has changed the color of the *hongjuui.*

2) Ritual Implements

The biggest change that occurred in ritual implements is that for *uijang,* used in the dance for *Jeongdaeeop,* which included thirty–five people in total : twenty–five for *gak, duk, go,* and *geum* in east, south, west, plus five–colored flags; five people for *na, gak, daeduk, daego,* and *daegeum;* and five for *jujakgi, cheongnyeonggi, hwangnyonggi, baekhogi,* and *hyeonmugi.* Judging from *Jongmyouigwe,* published in 1697, this was not featured during the time of King Sukjong. *Uijang* once more appears for *Jeongdaeeop* after the founding of the Korean Empire, but during Japanese occupation, *uijang* with thirty–five performers as well as *duk* as director of dance in *Botaepyeong* completely disappeared. This loss was never recovered, even with the revival of *Jongmyo jerye* in 1969 after the founding of the Republic.

The custom of dancers holding *yak* and *jeok* in *Botaepyeong* has been maintained since the time of the writing of *Gukjooryeui*. According to *Akhakgwebeom*, the length of the *jeok* handle is about 43.5cm and the *yuso* (流蘇, a tasseled ornament) is 45cm, feather, 6cm, and *hongnokcho* (紅綠綃, an ornament of red and green silk cloths), 15cm. The *jeok* we use today resembles that in *Akhakgwebeom*, except that the *hongnokcho* part has been changed to

Figure 37. Figures of *Jeok*

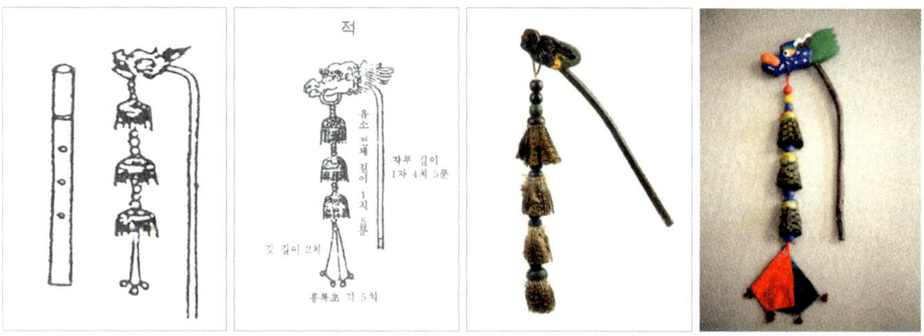

1 2 3 4

1 *Jeok* in *Gukjooryeui*
2 *Jeok* in *Akhakgwebeom*
3 *Jeok* housed in Jongmyo shrine
4 *Jeok* reproduced according to *Akhakgwebeom*

carved wood. The one preserved at the ancestral shrine has four *bang*, the part adorned with pheasant feathers. Since 2001, the Preservation Committee for *Jongmyo jeryeak* has revived *jeok* as recorded in *Akhakgwebeom*, and used it for the actual ritual ever since.

Meanwhile, the custom of holding swords, spears, bows and arrows in the *Jeongdaeeop* dance was practiced from the time of *Gukjooryeui* to 1917. After that, only swords and spears were used, without bows and arrows.

Akhakgwebeom records that "the sword is made of wood. Blade is enwrapped with silver foil and the hilt is covered with fish skin. Both *yangma* (陽亇, the edged rim between the blade and the hilt of a sword) and end of the hilt should be gilded with gold. For ribbon, a red string and green tassel are used. For the sword used in ancestral rituals, silver or gold should be avoided and it should not be painted in colors." Of the spear, it records, "the spear is made of wood. Hilt is red, adorned with deer horn at the bottom. Blade is enwrapped with silver foil, the tip of which is adorned with red tassel that looks like a flag. For the spear used in ancestral rituals, no silver foil is used but it is powdered and adorned with iron." The sword preserved at the ancestral shrine is painted blue at the blade and the hilt is not wrapped with fish skin. The sword is painted black at hilt and blade, with no red string attached. Since 2008, the Preservation Committee has been using swords and spears revived based on the records in *Akhakgwebeom*.

4 . The Symbolism of *Ilmu*

According to *Akgi*, "Saints created *ak* to answer to heaven, devised *ye* to respond to earth. With brightening of *ak* and *ye*, now heaven and earth are established." This stresses that *ak* should attend to heaven and *ye* to the earth.

According to *Akgi*, "Saints created *ak* to answer to heaven, devised *ye* to respond to earth. With brightening of *ak* and *ye*, now heaven and earth are established." This stresses that *ak* should attend to heaven and *ye* to the earth.

Ilmu is divided into *parilmu*, *yugilmu*, *sailmu*, and *iilmu*, and there are several theories as to the origin of the categories and their naming. One asserts that the status of the person offering the ritual should be represented by *jisu* (地數, lit., "earth numbers") which are 2, 4, 6, and 8. The number 8, as the greatest number of the earth, matches the subject in the highest rank of the ritual, and the lower numbers correspond to the lower ranks of subjects. Based on this theory, Duye of the Chinese Jin Dynasty ruled that *parilmu* should use sixty–four dancers in eight files and eight lines; *yugilmu*, thirty–six dancers in six files and six lines; *sailmu*, sixteen dancers in four files and four lines; and *iilmu*,

Figure 38. Figures of *Geom*, *chang*, and *gungsi*

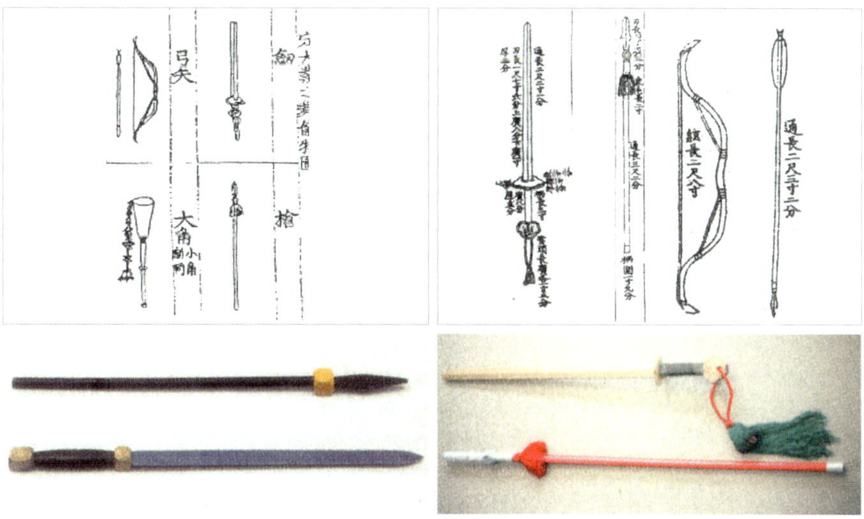

1	2
3	4

1 *Geom*, *chang*, and *gungsi* in *Gukjooryeui*
2 *Geom*, *chang*, and *gungsi* in *Akhakgwebeom*
3 *Geom* and *chang* housed in Jongmyo shrine
4 *Geom* and *chang* reproduced according to *Akhakgwebeom*

four dancers in two files and two lines.

Another theory is from Bokgeon of the Later Han Dynasty, asserting that "Dance is the doing of *palpung* (八風) using *pareum*, eight sounding materials, accordingly. *Pareum* are metal, stone, string, bamboo, gourd, earth, leather, and wood, and *palpung* refers to winds from eight directions." Based on this thinking, he placed eight dancers in each line, and depending on the number of lines, dance is labeled *parilmu*, *yugilmu*, *sailmu*, or *iilmu*. According to this theory, *parilmu* is danced with sixty–four dancers in eight files and eight lines; *yugilmu*, forty–eight dancers in six files and eight lines; *sailmu*, thirty–two dancers in eight files and four lines; and *iilmu*, sixteen dancers in eight files and two lines. "The doing of *palpung* using *pareum*" accordingly, means that musical instruments should sound harmonious and that dance should be danced in a way that spirits and men can unite, eight winds blow from all directions and everything in the universe lives in harmony. Therefore, the dance gestures in *ilmu* represent wind blowing softly from all directions.

The most important purpose of practicing the ancestral ritual with music in the early years of the Joseon Dynasty was to revive old customs by practicing proper music and etiquette which conformed to *Jurye*. The music played in ancestral rituals in Korea is grouped into two ensembles : the *deungga* and the *heonga*. On the stone platform is situated the *deungga* ensemble, and off the platform, the *heonga* ensemble. In the *jeonjeong* (前庭, front yard), between the two ensembles, *ilmu* should be performed. The *deungga* ensemble represents the movement of the sun, while the *heonga* ensemble symbolizes the Great Dipper constellation pointing towards Earth.

It is the principle of Samjae philosophy that the place of man is secured between heaven and earth. Man's affairs are largely divided into literary and military achievements. This is the reason that civil and military dances are presented between the two ensembles.

In the *Akmuuibo* (樂舞擬譜) section of volume nine of *Siakhwaseong* (詩樂和聲), it is written,

> Why is it that *ak* should always accompany dancing and that there must be civil and military dancing? The *heonga* ensemble symbolizes the stars pointing at the Earth and the *deungga* ensemble represents the sun answering to heaven. Between heaven and earth, there should be man and his achievements, in order to harmonize with heaven and earth. In discussing man's affairs, what is more comprehensive than military and literary achievements? This is the reason why we have placed our dancers south of *deungga* and north of *heonga*, situated between heaven and earth.

The *Botaepyeong* and *Jeongdaeeop* dances contain eleven movements each. In Yeongsin, the "Huimun" *Botaepyeong* dance is repeated nine times. During the Choheon–rye, *Botaepyeong* is danced in the nine movements between the first piece, "Huimun," and the last piece, "Yeokseong." In the Aheon–rye and Jongheon–rye, *ilmu* is danced to *Jeongdaeeop*, from "Somu" to "Yeonggwan.

This is all based on the writings of *Jurye* which stipulate : "If we danced dance of *unmun* (雲門) on New Year's eve at Wongu, changing music six times, the gods from heaven will all come down to receive our offerings." Thus, we dance six times for rituals offered to heaven. Then, it reads : "If we danced the dance of *hamji* (咸池) on a square hill surrounded by water, changing our music eight times, earth spirits will all come out to receive our offerings." Thus we dance eight times in rituals offered to the earth. Finally, it reads : "If we sang songs of *gudeok* (九德) and danced the dance of *guso* (九韶) in the middle of the ancestral shrine, changing our music nine times, we can present our offerings to human spirits." This is why dance in *Jongmyo jerye* is performed nine times.

In *Botaepyeong*, the dancer holds *yak* in the left hand and *jeok* in the right. *Yak*, according to the *pareum* system of *aak* instruments, belongs to the category of bamboo materials. It is a wind instrument with three finger holes, used not only as a musical instrument in the *deungga* and *heonga* ensembles in *aak* performance, but also as a ritual implement for *ilmu*. Moreover, the Chinese character for *yak* (龠) requires seventeen strokes to write, the highest number of strokes for a radical in Chinese and yet it is a character not broken down into lesser units. This indicates that the letter is one of the oldest characters in the Chinese language, shedding light on how old this musical instrument must be. Also, the three mouths, *gu* (口), inside the letter coincide with the three finger–holes of the *yak*, which symbolize creating harmony of all sound through these holes. From ancient times, the *yak* was made by cutting about 42cm of bamboo, grown in eastern grounds where the energy of spring is said to be the strongest. This is why it has represented the spirit of springtime. Furthermore, based on the similarity of pronunciation, *yak* would be regarded as the symbol of *ak* (樂).

Meanwhile, *jeok* is made from a wooden stick about 43.5cm long to which a dragon–head is attached as well as a *bang*, made with three bunches of pheasant feathers and wooden marbles. To this, *hongnokcho* with a knot, 15cm long, is attached. The entire instrument is about 45cm long. *Jeok* is made for *yong* (容, appearance). Both *yak* and *jeok* are dance implements, and the reason they are held this way is because the left hand represents movement and thus, *yang* and *ak*, while the right hand represents stillness, thus *yin* and *ye*. This is why the two are chosen to represent civil achievement.

Botaepyeong dance has the energy of *yang*, since it is performed by the *deungga* ensemble, symbolizing heaven. This dance, representing *yang*, is also subtle and beautiful. It begins with the posture of holding both hands to the chest and bowing, called *haphyung* (合胸), and it is with this same posture that the dance ends. It is the representative gesture for moderation, reverence, and modesty. Then, the right hand moves first, followed by the left hand, representing the union of *ye* and *ak*, and also the sun's motion. After that, while the two hands may move in parallel or be united again, the dancer dances to the left (the west) side first, then comes back to the center (representing the north), and then dances to the right (the east) and returns to the center again, expressing the movement of stars. Between expressing the movement of the sun and stars, or for closure, the dancer moves both arms symmetrically from top to bottom or left to right, expressing the soft breezes from the eight directions. These gestures represent the civil achievements of kings, which spread virtue, enrich all crops, and benefit mankind. Thus the dance, in all eleven sections, is very stylized, with each section having a particular motion.

Jeongdaeeop dance, on the other hand, is danced holding a sword or spear. It is danced to music played in *gyemyeon* mode by the *heonga* ensemble, which symbolizes the earth. Therefore, this dance has *yin* energy. The left hand, symbolizing *yang*, therefore does not hold anything and the dancer holds an implement only with his right hand, emphasizing that this dance is *yin*. In *ilmu* of *aak*, the left hand holds a *gan* and the right hand, *cheok*. In this case, *yin* is stressed by hitting *gan* with *cheok*. However, to leave the left hand empty and to hold a sword or spear in the right emphasizes *yin* even more. *Jeongdaeeop* dance, symbolizing yin, is complemented by the restrained movements of *yanggang* (陽剛, the state of strong *yang*).

"Somu," which is one of the movements of *Jeongdaeeop*, starts off with *haphyung* posture and the dancer draws his sword. After swinging the sword several times, the dancer dances in asymmetrical motions, then moves first to the left side, followed by symmetrical movements in a standing position. Then, he repeats the movements on the left and right sides. Unlike *Botaepyeong* dance that is very stylized overall, each of the eleven sections of *Jeongdaeeop* has its unique movements. Mostly, the dancer stands still, making symmetrical movements or dancing asymmetrically, emphasizing his left side by turning first before dancing on the right side repeatedly, to express various military deeds. Both *Botaepyeong* and *Jeongdaeeop* dances show harmonic balance between *yin* and *yang*, beautifully representing *palpung*, *palbang* (八方, eight directions), and *palgwae* (八卦, the eight trigrams for divinations).

5. The Procedure of *Ilmu*

Ilmu dancers are led in by the *jipsaaksa* (執事樂師, leader of musicians), following musicians of the *deungga* and *heonga* ensembles. They enter through the western gate to be positioned below the terrace, south of the *deungga* ensemble, west of the *sinno* (the main walkway in the yard), and north of the *heonga* ensemble. Then, they stand facing the north.

1) Yeongsin

The *jiprye* chants, "*heongajak botaepyeongjiak botaepyeongjimujak*" (軒架作保太平之樂保太平之舞作), and then the *heonga* ensemble repeatedly plays "Huimun" of *Botaepyeong* and dancers dance "Huimun" repeatedly. The rule is to play "Huimun" nine times, to welcome human spirits. However, since time runs short in our modern setting and since *heongwan* (獻官) and officiants are assigned for each chamber to make offerings, it is now rare to play "Huimun" nine times.

The signal for beginning and ending music would be given by the *jipsaaksa*, who is standing on the terrace. As the *jipsaaksa* calls "*deuo*," signaling the music to begin, a flag called *hwi* is raised. The *jipbagaksa* (執拍樂師, leading musician in charge of playing *bak*) strikes the *bak* once, followed by Gochuksamseong and then, after one more *bak*, "Huimun" will start, as well as *ilmu*. Since ritual and music occur simultaneously, when it is time to end, the *jipsa* must again say "*jio*." At this signal, the flag is lowered and then the *jipbagaksa* will strike the *bak* three times, and the *eo* is played three times. With this, the music ends and so will the dance. This is how music should start and end for Yeongsin, Jeonpye, Jinchan, and Choheon procedures. Together with the music, the dancing will start and finish as well.

2) Jeonpye

When the *jiprye* chants "*deunggajak botaepyeongjiak botaepyeongjimujak*" (登歌作保太平之樂保太平之舞作), the *deungga* ensemble repeatedly plays "Jeonpyehuimun" and *ilmu* dancers dance "Jeonpyehuimun."

3) Jinchan

The *jiprye* chants "*heongajak punganjiak*" (軒架作豊安之樂), and the *heonga* ensemble plays music for Jinchan with repeats. *Ilmu* is not danced at this time. To play music alone without dancing is the tradition of the Chinese Song Dynasty.

4) Choheon

The *jiprye* chants "*deunggajak botaepyeongjiak botaepyeongjimujak*" (登歌作保太平之樂保太平之舞作) and the *deungga* ensemble first plays "Huimun" of *Botaepyeong* as an introduction, followed by "Gimyeong," "Gwiin," "Hyeongga," "Jipnyeong," "Yunghwa," "Hyeonmi," "Yonggwang–

Jeongmyeong," "Junggwang," and "Daeyu." All these movements are accompanied by dancing. When the *jiprye* chants to stop the music, both the music and dance end.

The *daechuk* then recites a written prayer, followed by the *jiprye*, who signals to begin the music. Then *Jeolgosamtong* (節鼓三通), where the large drum is struck three times, follows and after that, the *bak* is struck once to begin the music. The first piece is "Gimyeong," followed by "Gwiin," "Hyeongga," "Jipnyeong," "Yunghwa," "Hyeonmi," "Yonggwang-Jeongmyeong," "Junggwang," and "Daeyu," with both music and dance. When the officiant comes out of the chamber, "Yeokseong," as music for the officiant's retreat from the chamber, is played and danced.

The *jiprye* then chants "*botaepyeongjimutoe jeongdaeeopjimujin*" (保太平之舞退定大業之舞進) and the dancers bend down to put down their *yak* and *jeok* implements for the civil dance, and pick up wooden swords and spears to dance the military dance. The four front rows hold swords, while the back four rows hold spears. In principle, *Botaepyeong* dancers should exit to let military dancers in. However, since we do not have enough dancers today, the same dancers perform both civil and military dances.

5) Aheon

The *jiprye* chants "*heongajak jeongdaeeopjiak jeongdaeeopjimujak*" (軒架作定大業之樂定大業之舞作), and the *jipsa* signals, saying "*deuo*," to order the flag to be raised. Then, the *heonga* ensemble, using the signaling pattern of

Jingosiptong, Gochuksamseong, and one strike of *bak*, plays "Somu" as music for the officiant's entrance into the chamber. This is followed by "Dokgyeong," "Takjeong," "Seonwi," "Sinjeong," "Bunung," "Suneung," "Chongyu," "Jeongse," and "Hyeokjeong" in music and dance. When the officiant comes out of the sacred room, "Yeonggwan," as music for retreat from the chamber, is played and danced. To end, the *jipsa* calls out "*jio*," followed by three beats of the *bak* and *eo*.

6) Jongheon

The *jiprye* calls out "*heongajak jeongdaeeopjiak jeongdaeeopjimujak*" (軒架作定大業之樂定大業之舞作), and the *jipsa* says "*deuo*." The flag is raised, followed by Jingosamtong at the *heonga* ensemble. The *bak* is struck once to begin "Somu" as music for the entrance of the officiant. Then, the *heonga* ensemble plays, in the order of "Dokgyeong," "Takjeong," "Seonwi," "Sinjeong," "Bunung," "Suneung," "Chongyu," "Jeongse," and "Hyeokjeong," along with dancing. When the officiant is out of the chamber, "Yeonggwan," as music for retreat, is played. Then, to finish the music, the *jipsa* says "*jio*," the *bak* is struck three times, and the *eo* is rubbed three times. This is followed by Daegeumsipcha as finale.

7) Cheolbyeondu and Songsin

For Cheolbyeondu, the *deungga* ensemble plays "Onganjiak," and for

Songsin, the *heonga* ensemble plays "Heunganjiak," but with no dancing, following the tradition of the Chinese Song Dynasty.

6 . *Ilmu* Notation

Dance notation for *ilmu* in Jongmyo comprise *Siyongmubo* (時用舞譜, *Current Dance Notation*) and the notation used at Yiwangjik aakbu since the 1930s. Comparing these two sources with *Sejo sillok*, *Daeakhubo*, and *Sogagwonbo*, the *Siyong botaepyeongjimu* (時用保太平之舞, the *Botaepyeong* dance of today) of *Siyongmubo* is identical to that of *Daeakhubo*, and *Siyong jeongdaeeopjimu* (時用定大業之舞, the *Jeongdaeeop* dance of today) is the same as that in *Sejo sillok*, while the 1930's version is the same as *Sogagwonbo*. *Daeakhubo* was published in 1759, the thirty–fifth year of King Yeongjo's reign, in which the music of King Sejong's time was compiled. Therefore, we can assume that *Siyongmubo* was compiled during the time of King Yeongjo and King Jeongjo, which was after the compilation of *Daeakhubo*.

Siyongmubo divides a page into four columns; each column is divided into six beats (one per square). Each column also has an additional, narrow column beside it for Oeumyakbo or Gungsanghabo (宮上下譜), with the wide space in–between used to insert drawings and instructions for dance movements. When we compare the dance notation for *Siyong botaepyeongjimu* of *Siyongmubo* to *Daeakhubo*, we can see that one entire page is missing, from the fourth to eleventh columns of "Gwiin," eight columns in total.

Comparing *Siyong jeongdaeeopjimu* of *Siyongmubo* to notation in *Sejo sillok*, while "Hyeokjeong" has thirteen columns and "Yeonggwan" has eight columns in *Sejo sillok*, "Hyeokjeong" has fourteen columns and "Yeonggwan" is omitted from *Siyongmubo*. This means that one column of "Hyeokjeong" in *Siyong jeongdaeeopjimu* of *Siyongmubo* and six columns in the beginning part of "Yeonggwan" are missing, comprising an omission of one whole page.

In the notation from the 1930s, all the missing parts of *Siyongmubo* were recovered by Kim Yeong–je (金寧濟), director of *aak* at the time, complemented with explanatory instructions. *Siyongmubo* only has word descriptions alongside drawings, with no explanation as to dance movements. However, in 1956, Yi Ju–hwan (李珠煥), the first president of the National Gugak Center,

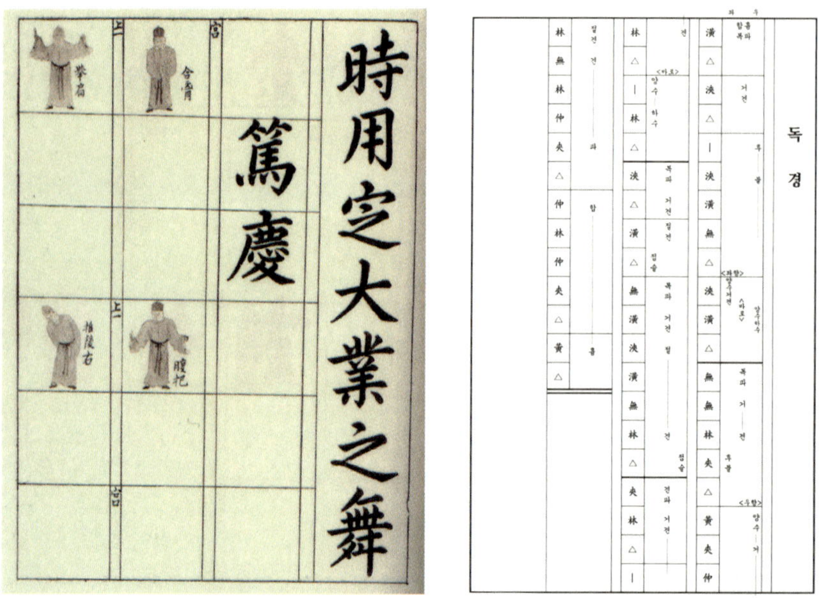

Figure 39 . *Siyongmubo* (left) and current dance notation (right)

wrote "Siyongmuyonghaeje" (時用舞譜解題, Explanation for Siyongmubo) in the first volume of *Minsokhakbo* (民俗學報), in which Kim Yeong–je's explanation of dance movements were included; this gave us some clues in understanding how the dance proceeded in specific detail.

The dance notation of the 1930's has been transmitted from Aakbuwon yangseongso (雅樂部員養成所, Training School for *Aak* Musicians), an institute affiliated with Yiwangjik aakbu, through Gugaksa yangseongso (國樂士養成所, Training School for Musicians of Korean Traditional Music), an organization affiliated with the National Gugak Center, and to the Gugak National High School, all the way to the present. It contains explanatory notes for dance movements for a better understanding, and, between Jeongganbo for dance notation, pitches for *pyeonjong* and *pyeongyeong* are recorded. In the wider space between, instructions for dance are provided, written using dotted lines to show music and the flow of durational values.

The Aesthetic of *Jongmyo jeryeak* : Its Ideological Background and Aesthetic Characteristics

The Aesthetic of *Jongmyo jeryeak* : Its Ideological Background and Aesthetic Characteristics

Jongmyo jeryeak, in its ideological background, is based on Confucianism. Confucianism exists in many schools, such as Gyeonghak (經學, the Study of Confucian Classics), Seongnihak (性理學, Neo–Confucianism), and Silhak(實學, Practical Learning), but that which underlies *Jongmyo jeryeak* is a combination of many ancient cultural traditions.[1] More specifically, among Confucian teachings, *Jongmyo jeryeak* is based on Yeangnon (禮樂論, Theory of Rites and Music), Samjaeron (三才論, Theory of Three Principals), Junghwaron (中和論, Theory of Harmony), and Eumyang ohaengnon (陰陽五行論, Theory of *Yin* and *Yang*, and the Five Elements).

1) Yi Suk–hi, "Akhakgwebeom sasangchegyeui hyeongseong baegyeonggwa seonggyeok," *Hangugeumaksahakbo* Vol. 33 (2004) : 127–50.

1. Ideological Background

1) Yeangnon (禮樂論, Theory of Rites and Music)

Yeangnon aims to create harmony between rites and music, so that they complement each other in order to form the basis for political, social, and cultural rules. According to *Yegi*, the relationship between rites and music is explained in the dichotomies of outside/inside, difference/same, conflict/harmony, justice/benevolence, and repaying/giving.

It was the Chinese tradition to accompany *Ye* (禮) with music. In an offering ritual during the Chinese Zhou Dynasty, food, greetings, wine, music, dance, and singing would be presented according to their ritualistic procedures, in order to appease and entertain the gods. Among these, wine, music, and dance were considered the most important, and thus were called the Three Important Events. Therefore, we could say that playing during a ritual was originally unrelated to Confucian teaching, but as time went by and as the theory of rites and music was systemized, it become absorbed into Confucian tradition. Thus, the playing of music during *Jongmyo jerye* is derived from such a theory. With Yeangnon as their foundation, the theory of three principals, the theory of harmony, and the theory of *yin* and *yang*, and the five elements provide more specific ideological background.

2) Samjaeron (三才論, Theory of Three Principals)

Samjae refers to heaven, earth, and man–the basic units and elements of change in the universe. According to *Yeokgyeong* (易經, *Classic of Changes*; also known as *Juyeok* (周易), *Book of Changes*) divination, heaven is established by *yin* and *yang*, the earth by sturdiness and gentleness, and man by benevolence. In a Confucian court ritual, the subjects for the ritual are divided into heaven, earth, and man. Gods of heaven include the sky, wind, clouds, and rain, and gods of earth are ground and crops, while human gods include all former kings, queens, and great scholars. A rite offered to heaven is called *je* (祭), to earth, *sa* (祀), and to man, *hyang* (享).

Through such Samjaeron theory, the mode of the music, the number of performers, and the color of instruments are determined. For example, *Botaepyeong* and *Jeongdaeeop* were originally in *imjong pyeongjo* and *namryeo gyemyeonjo* modes, respectively. However, after they were included into *Jongmyo jeryeak*, they changed to *cheonghwangjong pyeongjo* and *cheonghwangjong gyemyeonjo* modes. This follows the theory of Samjaeron that human gods should be served with the modes starting with Hwangjong as tonic. Additionally, following the principle of playing nine times for human gods, in music for the Yeongsin procedure, "Yeongsinhuimun" is played nine times. For instrumentation, *nogo* and *nodo* painted in red were used for rites offered to human gods in the *heonga* ensemble. These are all examples of following the rules designated for rites paying homage to human gods and, therefore, the Theory of Three Principals.

3) Junghwaron (中和論, Theory of Harmony)

In *Akseo,* it is stated that, according to the *Chungwan* section of *Jurye,* since the three tonic notes are all in the middle range of sound, the music of heaven should use Hyeopjong (E^b), representing the month of February in the lunar calendar, as tonic; the music of man should apply Hwangjong (C), representing the month of November in the lunar calendar, as tonic; and the music of earth should employ Yubin ($F^\#$), representing the month of May in the lunar calendar, as tonic. However, since it is June when the energy of earth is strong, Imjong (G), representing the month of June in the lunar calendar, should be in use as tonic instead of Yubin which is not appropriate as tonic for earth.

"Junghwa" refers to the nature of music, of how it affects the world, and terms for making good music. *Jung* (中) means "not excessive," and *hwa* (和) implies "everything is in proper order." Therefore, Junghwa signifies the "righteous thing" and "harmony," and thus what constitutes musical principles and how they affect people. The influence of music can be examined from two dimensions : individual and society. For an individual, music straightens one's heart, and for society, it is edifying. According to the preface of *Akhakgwebeom*, music makes the human heart beat faster, enlightens people's spirits, and clears their minds. This refers to the function of music to cleanse the human heart. Also, in *Akhakgwebeom*, it is stated that "Principles of *ak* are intimately related to ruling the people," and this relates to the social function of music. Such social meaning of music has been stressed since ancient times. In *Yegi*, there is a passage stating that music will make people good, move their hearts, and change customs. The reason that music acts this way is because of its nature, of Junghwa.

This concept of Junghwa later developed into a philosophical issue in Neo–Confucianism during the Chinese Song Dynasty. *Jungyong* (中庸, *The Doctrine of the Mean*) offers a more specific description of this : "Not to show emotion is called *jung* and *hwa* is when everything falls properly in its place." Scholars of the Chinese Song Dynasty adopted the book, *The Doctrine of the Mean*, as one of the four major books. They connected Junghwa in relation to the heart, disposition, and emotions, saying that *jung* and *hwa* are the relations between disposition and emotions, that the heart controls disposition and emotions, and that Junghwa is the virtue of human nature.[2] *Jongmyo jeryeak*, as it follows the tradition of rites and music, is fundamentally based on the Theory of Harmony.

4) Eumyang ohaengnon (陰陽五行論, Theory of *Yin* and *Yang*, and the Five Elements)

Yin and *yang* are the two contrasting natures that constitute the basis of our world, and the five elements refer to the features of materials in nature. *Yin* and *yang*, and the five elements, have existed as two separate entities but came to be combined into a single theory by Jujahakpa (朱子學派, scholars

2) Yi Suk–hi, *ibid*.

following the doctrine of Chu–tzu (朱熹, 1130–1200). Ju Ryeom–gye (周敦頤, 1017–1073) of the Song Dynasty combined the sentence, "*Yeogyutaegeuk* (易有太極) *sisaengyangui* (是生兩儀)" (because of the abundance of energy within *taiji*, it began to move and thus produced *yin* and *yang*) from the *Book of Changes* with the theory of the Five Elements, and came up with a theory on the origin of the universe which proceeds in the order of *taiji*, *yin* and *yang*, five elements, and all creation.

According to this, *taiji* is moved and begets the *yang*. When the movement reaches its maximum, it becomes tranquil again. Tranquility, when it reaches its extreme, will become movement again. One movement and one tranquility will form a root, dividing into *yin* and *yang*, from which are constructed heaven and earth. The changes of *yang* and combination of *yin* beget water, fire, metal, wood, and earth. The five energies will move properly, causing time to flow forward. The five elements are *yin* and *yang*; *yin* and *yang* is a type of *taiji*; and *taiji* is originally the endlessness. Now, we will discuss how such a theory of *yin* and *yang*, and the five elements is reflected in *Jongmyo jeryeak*, focusing on instrumentation, the number of repetitions, and the types of ritual implements.

a. Elements of *Yin* and *Yang*

Aak, in general, features two ensembles called the *deungga* and *heonga* ensembles, which is also the case for *Jongmyo jeryeak*. The *deungga* and *heonga* ensembles must, in principle, use musical modes that coincide with *yin* and *yang* theory. However, since *Jongmyo jeryeak* is not *aak*, it does not follow this rule.

Nevertheless, *Botaepyeong* and *Jeongdaeeop* were created based on the theory of *yin* and *yang*. *Botaepyeong* is praise of the civil achievements of kings and thus belongs to *yang*. From numbers one to five, called *saengsu* (生數, lit., "living number"), the *yang* numbers which are one, three, and five are added to become nine, *noyangsu* (老陽數, lit., "aged *yang* number"), which represents *yang*. Also, in *Botaepyeong*, the dance changes nine times. On the other hand, *Jeongdaeeop* praises military achievements, and therefore, *yin*. The number six, as the sum of the two *yin* numbers two and four from the *saengsu*, is the *noeumsu* (老陰數, lit., "aged *yin* number"), representing *yin*. In *Jeongdaeeop*, the dance changes six times. Thus, as *Botaepyeong* and *Jeongdaeeop* were included into *Jongmyo jeryeak*, according to the principle of nine sounds, the number of complete movements is nine, except for movements used at the beginning and end for the entrance and retreat from the chambers of the officiants making offerings.

b. Theory of Five Elements

In rites offered to gods of heaven, *Gangsinak* (降神樂, music for calling the gods) in *hyeopjonggung* mode is played six times. For rites offered to earth gods, *Gangsinak* in *imjonggung* mode is played eight times, while for rites offered to human gods, *Gangsinak* in *hwangjonggung* mode is played nine times. In summary, performing the pieces six times for heaven, eight times for earth, and nine times for humans are the application of *sipgan* (十干, Ten Heavenly Stems)[3] and *sibiji* (十二支, Twelve Earthly Branches),[4] which is a type of five–elements theory.

Hyeopjong, as tonic in the rites for heavenly gods, corresponds with the *myo* rank of the *sibiji* and *jeong* position in terms of *sipgan*, and it implies the number six. Imjong, as tonic for earthly gods, indicates the *mi* rank of the *sibiji* and *eul* position in *sipgan*, and its number is eight. Hwangjong, as tonic for human spirits, is the *ja* rank of the *sibiji* and *gap* position in *sipgan*, and its number is nine. *Jongmyo jeryeak*, performing "Yeongsinhuimun" nine times in Yeongsin, follows the number for human spirits. This illustrates that the number of performances in Yeongsin has been determined by the Theory of Five Elements based on the Theory of Three Principals.

Today, the ritual implements used in *ilmu* for *Jongmyo jerye* are *yak* and *jeok* for *Botaepyeong*, and *geom* and *chang* for *Jeongdaeeop*. However, in the early years of the Joseon Dynasty, when *Botaepyeong* and *Jeongdaeeop* had just been included into the ritual, there were seventy–one musicians, thirty–six dancers, and thirty–five handlers of ritual implements for *Jeongdaeeop* only. Ritual implements include musical instruments and flags.

Flags for *Jeongdaeeop* are *obanggi* (五方旗, five–cardinal point flags) and *osaekgi* (五色旗, five–colored flags). *Osaekgi* include *hwanggi* (yellow flag), *cheonggi* (blue flag), *baekgi* (white flag), *heukgi* (black flag), and *honggi* (red flag), which together are what is called *obangsaek* (五方色, colors of five cardinal points), representing the principle of the five elements. These five–

3) *Sipgan* or Ten Heavenly Stems are *gap* (甲), *eul* (乙), *byeong* (丙), *jeong* (丁), *mu* (戊), *gi* (己), *gyeong* (庚), *sin*(辛), *im* (壬), and *gye* (癸). The Heavenly Stems are used in combination with the Earthly Branches to produce a compound sexagenary cycle.

4) *Sibiji* or Twelve Earthly Branches are *ja* (子), *chuk* (丑), *in* (寅), *myo* (卯), *jin* (辰), *sa* (巳), *o* (午), *mi* (未), *sin*(申), *yu* (酉), *sul* (戌), and *hae* (亥).

colored flags are placed in five directions, black for north, red for south, blue for east, white for west, and yellow for the center.

Obanggi, on the other hand, includes *cheongnyonggi, baekhogi, jujakgi, hyeonmugi*, and *hwangnyonggi*. These flags not only represent the five directional hues but also messenger gods for each cardinal point. The *sasin* (四神) refer to the guards of the four directions : *cheongnyong*(blue dragon) in the east, *baekho* (white tiger) in the west, *jujak* (red phoenix) in the south, and *hyeonmu* in the north. Ancient people thought these four animals were gods of the four directions, assigning them the four seasons : blue dragon for spring, white tiger for fall, red phoenix for summer, and *hyeonmu* for winter. They used this to decide where to build their capital city. In *Jeongdaeeop*, they added *hwangnyonggi*, making it an even more faithful representation of the five elements. Thus, *obanggi* with images of the *sasin* and *hwangnyong* (yellow dragon) embody five–elements teaching. Since *Jongmyo jeryeak* was created based on the principle of *yin* and *yang*, and the five elements, we may assume that it constitutes the ideological basis of this ritual, although the current *Jongmyo jeryeak* has lost these features.

2. Aesthetic Characteristics

The nature of beauty appearing in *Jongmyo jeryeak* can be understood in two aspects : abstract beauty arising from its history and background, and realistic beauty that comes from within itself. The abstract beauty of *Jongmyo jeryeak* can be described as "transcendental beauty," while the realistic beauty can be termed "dynamic beauty."

1) Beauty Arising from Transcendence

Transcendence in this case means transcending ordinary boundaries of time, space, and mind. The transcendence of time found in *Jongmyo jeryeak* has to do with its long history. Space is transcended too, since a separate, holy space has been provided for the ritual. Transcendence in the mind arises from man's sincere attempt to get in touch with the spirits.

Botaepyeong and *Jeongdaeeop* in *Jongmyo jeryeak* have been continuously transmitted throughout six hundred years of Korean history. *Jongmyo jeryeak* has survived political turmoil, including the Imjinwaeran, Byeongjahoran, Japanese Colonialization, and the Korean War, undergoing change as an integral part of the lives of the people. Therefore, it came to acquire a kind of aloof beauty, not easily shaken or broken. We may thus assert that one of the important elements in discussing the beauty of *Jongmyo jeryeak* is its historicity, acquired through time, and internalized in its music after such a long history fraught with events.

Jongmyo jeryeak is music performed within the space of the ancestral shrine. It is a sacred place, in which tablets of past kings and queens are placed. The simplicity of its surroundings, with repeated patterns in buildings and the empty foreground, help make it seem even more numinous. The mystical feeling that arises when such an environment is filled with sacred music is what constitutes the transcendental beauty of *Jongmyo jeryeak*.

The ancestral ritual is the ground to act out "filial piety," and therefore requires utmost care from the descendants. When performing the ritual, the offering agents must bow most reverently. Musicians and dancers take great care not to miss even the slightest detail. Such sincerity of mind and heart in the offering parties provide transcendental beauty to the event. With a backdrop consisting of the spacious and sacred ground of the ancestral shrine, the slow but grand melody of "Jeonpyehuimun" is echoed, followed by the long, grim sonority of *taepyeongso* in movements "Somu," "Bunung," and "Yeonggwan." These are what represent the transcendental beauty unique to *Jongmyo jeryeak*.

2) Dynamic Beauty

Jongmyo jeryeak features a dynamic beauty akin to a flowing river, arising from many factors including orchestration, instruments, and musical mode. The feeling of dynamic movement in *Jongmyo jeryeak* springs from being thoroughly faithful to form. *Jongmyo jeryeak* features both music and dance. Music is provided by the *deungga* and *heonga* ensembles, and there are two types of dance, civil and military, performed in alternation. There is a strict rule as to when and what type of music and dance should be performed, and by whom. Performers are thoroughly trained so that everything proceeds as programmed. During the brief moments where beginning and ending patterns are played, using the percussion instruments *bak, chuk, eo, jingo, jeolgo,* and *jing*, the formula of tension and release is repeated. *Ilmu* in *Jongmyo jeryeak* does not feature large bodily movements. Sixty–four dancers moving exactly the same in a most restrained fashion produce a strong impression of dynamism found nowhere else. Thus, in *Jongmyo jeryeak*, strict formalism is one important factor in creating dynamic beauty.

Botaepyeong and *Jeongdaeeop* were originally in *imjong pyeongjo* and *namryeo gyemyeonjo* modes, respectively, but were changed to *cheonghwangjong pyeongjo* and *cheonghwangjong gyemyeonjo* modes. The resulting rise in pitch has made both movements sound much grander and more energetic. This is especially true when the *dochang*, the male singer, chants his high–pitched *akjang*. In *Jongmyo jeryeak*, it is the *dangpiri* that plays the main melody. The *dangpiri* is unable to play intricate embellishing notes, so the melody sounds very simple and straightforward. This is what makes *Jongmyo jeryeak* sound masculine and dynamic. In summary, *Jongmyo jeryeak* features perfect formalism, keen musical timbre, and well–restrained dance, making it one of the most dynamic art forms in Korean culture.

Performing Costumes and Implements of *Jongmyo jeryeak*

Performing Costumes and Implements of *Jongmyo jeryeak*

Based on a number of written sources on ritual attire, the costumes for *Jongmyo jeryeak* can be assigned to three stylistic periods : the fifteenth century, the seventeenth to nineteenth century, and the late nineteenth century forward. Attire for *Jongmyo jeryeak* in the fifteenth century is recorded is *Gukjooryeui* and *Akhakgwebeom*; seventeenth to nineteenth century style is documented in *Jongmyouigwe*, *Chungwantonggo*, and *Jeungbomunheonbigo* (增補文獻備考, *Expanded Edition of the Korean Encyclopedia of Documents and Institutions*); and the style after the nineteenth century is found in *Joseonakgaeyo*. *Akhakgwebeom*, *Jongmyouigwe*, and *Joseonakgaeyo* also contain visual illustrations.

Akhakgwebeom provides a prototype for *Jongmyo jeryeak* performers' attire and *Jongmyouigwe* shows its developed form in the early eighteenth century, while *Joseonakgaeyo* offers us the roots of the present–day costume. The attire differs, depending on the role of the performer, of which there are five types: *aksa* (present–day *jipbak*, or clapper holder), *akgong* (present–day *aksa*, musicians), *ilmu akgong* (dancers) for *Botaepyeong* and *Jeongdaeeop*, and *jipsaaksa*. We shall examine the costumes for *aksa*, *akgong*, and *ilmu akgong* in more detail.

1. Costume of *Aksa* (*Jipbak*, Clapper Holder)

1) *Aksa* Attire for *Jongmyo jeryeak* in *Akhakgwebeom*

Akhakgwebeom records that the costume for *aksa* in *Jongmyo jeryeak* consisted of *bokdu*, *nokchosam* (綠綃衫, green–colored robe), *ojeongdae* (烏鞓帶, belt for the formal robes of musicians), and *heukpihwa* (黑皮靴, black–colored half–boots for government officials in formal attire).

Figure 40. *Aksa* attire in *Akhakgwebeom*

Bokdu

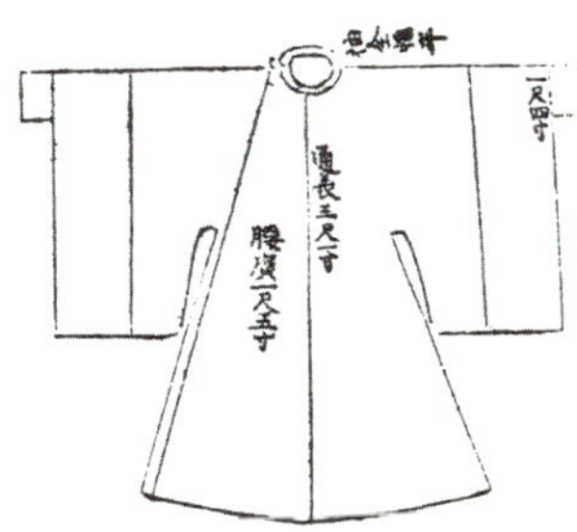

Nokchosam

Ojeongdae

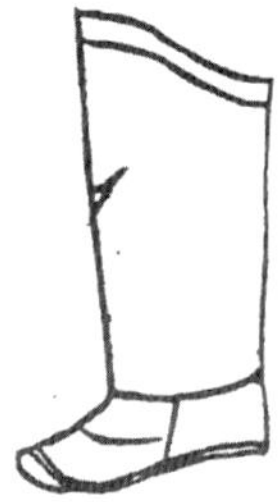

Heukpihwa

2) *Aksa* Attire for *Jongmyo jeryeak* in *Jongmyouigwe*

Jongmyouigwe records that the costume for *aksa* in *Jongmyo jeryeak* consisted of *bokdu, nokchosam, ojeongdae,* and *heukpihwa*; not much different from that found in *Akhakgwebeom*.

Figure 41. *Aksa* attire in *Jongmyouigwe*

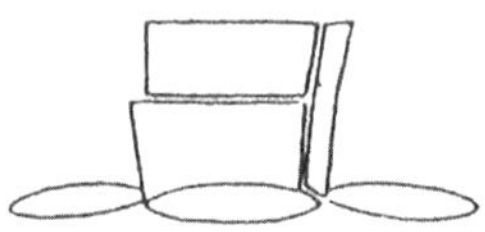

Bokdu

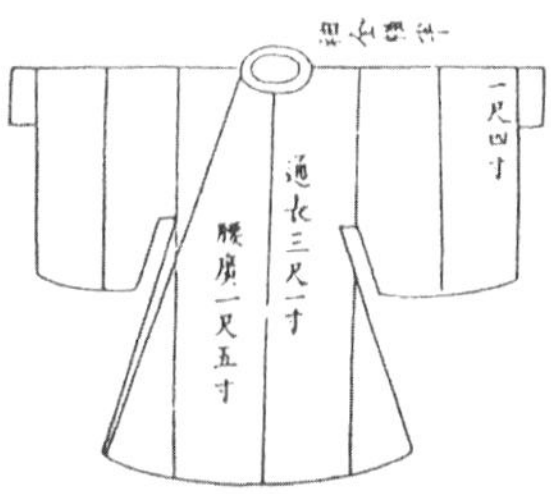

Nokchosam

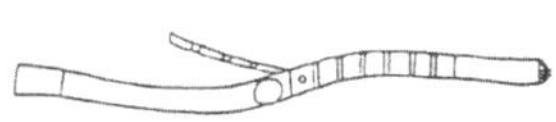

Ojeongdae

Baekpomal

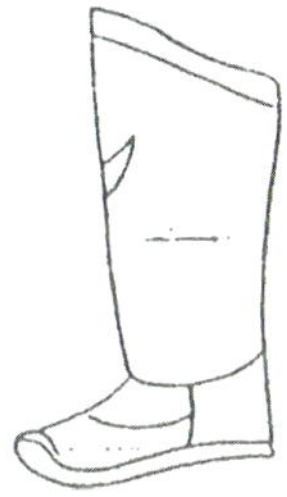

Heukpihwa

3) *Aksa* Attire from the Korean Empire to the Present

No record remains of the *aksa*'s costume from the founding of the Korean Empire until Japanese occupation. What *aksa* wear today is not too different from what was known until the late nineteenth century. Differences from *Akhakgwebeom* and *Jongmyouigwe* are that *hyungbae* (胸背, embroidered ornaments in square shape attached to the chest and back of the robe) are added and *gakdae* (角帶, belt for the government officials) is used, instead of *ojeongdae*. Also, *nokchosam* is called *cheongsam* (青衫, lit., "blue robe") and *heukpihwa* is named *mokhwa*.

Figure 42. Current *aksa* attire

2 . Costume of *Akgong* in the *Deungga* and *Heonga* Ensembles

1) *Akgong* Attire for *Jongmyo jeryeak* in *Akhakgwebeom*

Attire for musicians in the *deungga* and *heonga* ensembles during the time of *Akhakgwebeom* comprised *gaejeok* (介幘, headband), *biransam* (翡鸞衫, red silk robe for musicians), *baekjujungdan* (白紬中單, white–silk inner–robe for musicians), *baekchodae* (白綃帶, belt for the formal robe for musicians), *baekpomal*, and *opiri*. According to *Akhakgwebeom*, the *gaejeok* is made by laminating papers, and the *byeona* (邊兒, outer rim) is formed with wire. Inside, fine hemp cloth is pasted which is then painted black and gold. Finally, a blue silk ribbon is attached. *Biransam* is made of red silk, with the image of a phoenix placed on the front, back, and both shoulders. *Baekjujungdan* is made by weaving refined white silk, biased with black silk. *Baekjumaldae* (白紬抹帶, belt for the musicians' attire) is also made from woven fine white silk cloth.

Figure 43. *Aksa* attire in *Jongmyouigwe*

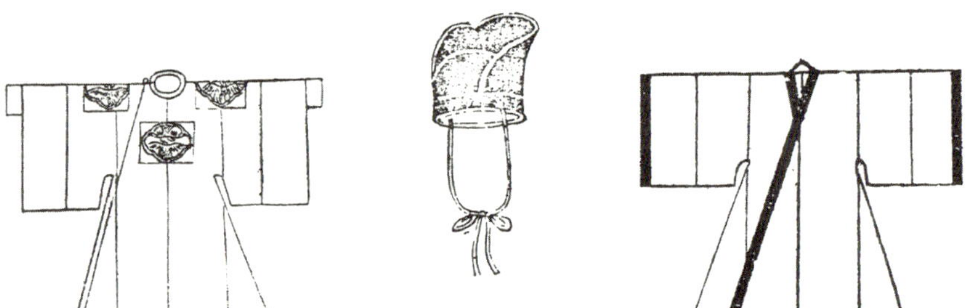

Gaejeok

Biransam *Baekjujungdan*

Baekjumaldae

Baekpomal

Opiri

2) *Akgong* Attire for *Jongmyo jeryeak* in *Jongmyouigwe*

According to *Jongmyouigwe*, the *deungga* and *heonga* ensemble musicians' costume comprised *gaejeok, hongjuui, baekchodae, baekpomal,* and *opiri*. During the time of *Jongmyouigwe*, *biransam* was replaced by *hongjuui*; this remains today. Unlike *biransam*, the *hongjuui* no longer has a pattern on the chest, back, and shoulders. The overall design also shifted from *sam* (衫) to *ui* (衣), and therefore the musicians' attire became identical to that of the *ilmu*

Figure 44. *Akgong* attire in *Jongmyouigwe*

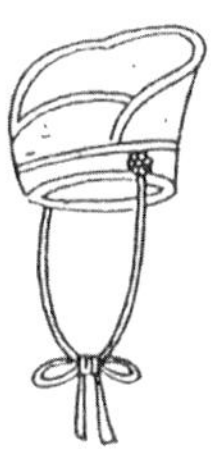

Gaejeok

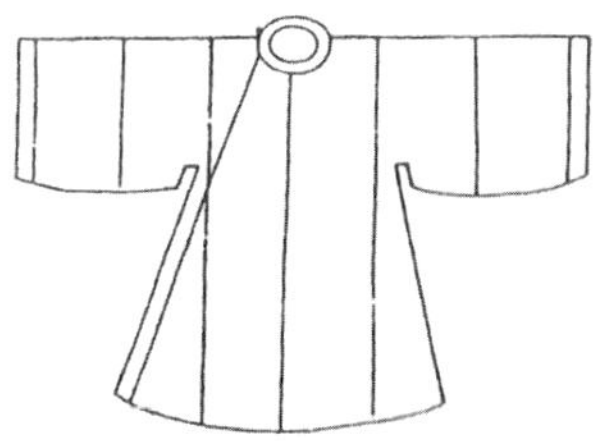

Hongjuui

Baekchodae

Baekpomal

Opiri

dancers in shape, although different in color. Finally, the *baekjujungdan*, a sort of undergarment, has vanished.

3) From 1892 to the Present

Musician's attire for *Jongmyo jeryeak* was renewed in 1892; however, this meant little more than a change in the belt, from *baekchodae* to *namsadae*. We can confirm this from drawings in "Jongmyochinjegyujedoseol" (宗廟親祭規制圖說, referring to a folding screen by this name), dating from the late nineteenth century, on which the musician is wearing a dark blue or black belt instead of a white *baekchodae*. This renewed form was maintained until the time of the Korean Empire, and even until 1917. Present–day attire for the musicians consists of *gaejeok*, *hongjuui*, *namsadae*, and *mokhwa*, faithfully following the 1892 version.

Figure 45. *Akgong* in the *heonga* ensemble in "Jongmyochinjegyujedoseol" (left)
Enlarged picture of *akgong* (right)

Figure 46.
Current musicians' attire
for *Jongmyo jerye*

3 . Costume of *Botaepyeong* Dancers

1) Attire for *Botaepyeong* Dancers in *Akhakgwebeom*

Akhakgwebeom writes that the costume for *ilmu* dancers in *Botaepyeong* consisted of *jinhyeongwan, namjuui, jeoksang* (赤裳, red skirt), *jeokmaldae, baekpomal,* and *opiri.*

Figure 47. Attire for *Botaepyeong* dancers in *Akhakgwebeom*

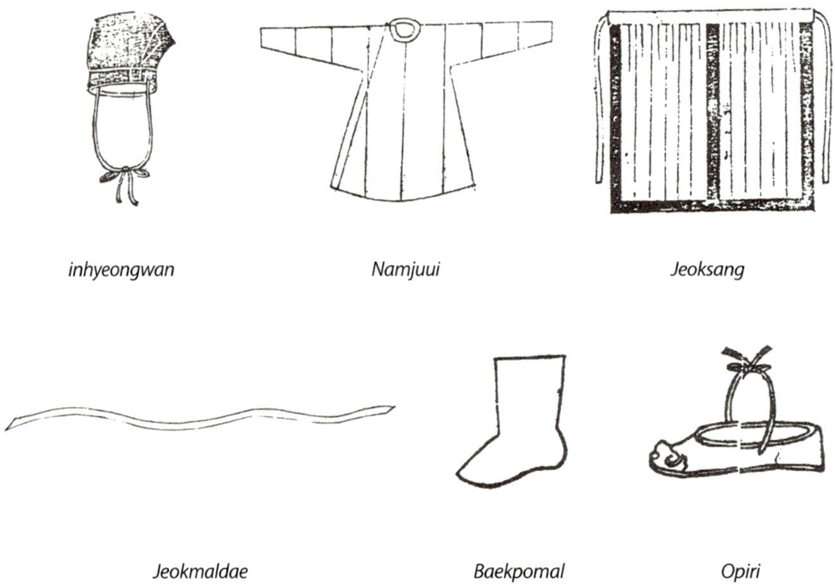

2) Attire for *Botaepyeong* Dancers in *Jongmyouigwe*

Jongmyouigwe records that attire for *ilmu* dancers comprised *jinhyeongwan, namjuui, jeoksang, jeokmaldae, baekpomal,* and *opiri*–the same as documented in *Akhakgwebeom*.

Thus, compared to musicians' outfits, dance attire experienced less change. The design in this period was maintained until the end of the Joseon period, which can be confirmed by images appearing on the folding screen, "Jongmyochinjegyujedoseol" and in *Siyongmubo*. The outer skirt was worn over the robe before the time of King Yeongjo and King Jeongjo, but was

Figure 48. Attire for *Botaepyeong* dancers in *Jongmyouigwe*

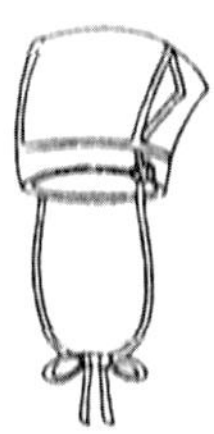

Jinhyeongwan

Namjuui

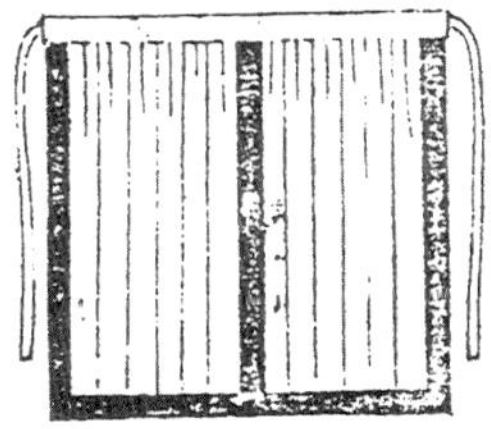

Jeoksang

Jeokmaldae

Baekpomal

Opiri

Figure 49. *Munmu* attire in "Jongmyochinjegyujedoseol" (left)
Figure 50. *Munmu* attire in *Siyongmubo* (right)

subsequently moved underneath. If the dancer in *Siyongmubo* was thus wearing a skirt, he was probably wearing it beneath his robe.

3) From the Korean Empire to the Present

Present–day attire for *ilmu* dancers in *Jongmyo jeryeak* shows that the costume consisted of *bokdu, hongjuui, namsadae,* and *mokhwa,* the first record of which appears in *Joseonakgaeyo* in 1897. Therefore, what present–day dancers of *ilmu* are wearing can be traced back to the founding of the Korean Empire. In this period, instead of *jinhyeongwan*, dancers wore *bokdu,* and *hongjuui* rather than *namjuui.* Also, the skirt is nowhere to be found, and *namsadae* is worn instead of *jeokmaldae*. Thus, the traditional unique attire for *ilmu* dancers in *Botaepyeong* has disappeared and grown closer to that for the musicians.

Figure 51. Current *munmu* attire for *Jongmyo jeryeak*

4 . Costume of *Jeongdaeeop* Dancers

1) Attire for *Jeongdaeeop* Dancers in *Akhakgwebeom*

According to *Akhakgwebeom*, *ilmu* dancers wore *pibyeon*, *namjuui*, *jeoksang*, *jeokmaldae*, *baekpomal*, and *opiri* for *Jeongdaeeop*. This is identical to the outfit for *ilmu* dancers in *Botaepyeong*, except for the hat.

Figure 52. Attire for *Jeongdaeeop* dancers in *Akhakgwebeom*

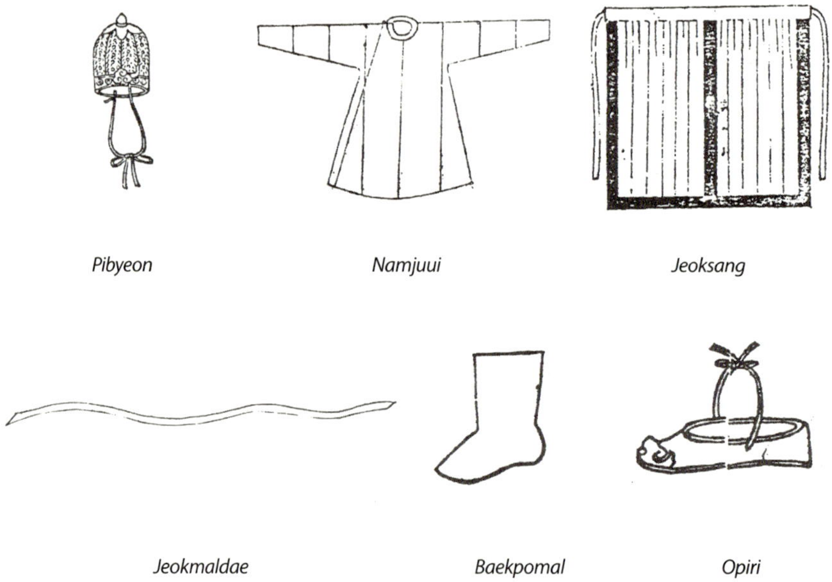

2) Attire for *Jeongdaeeop* Dancers in *Jongmyouigwe*

In the latter part of the Joseon period, attire for *ilmu* dancers in *Jeongdaeeop*, as recorded in *Jongmyouigwe* and *Chungwantonggo*, comprised *pibyeon, namjuui, jeoksang, jeokmaldae, baekpomal*, and *opiri*, which does not differ from what is found in *Akhakgwebeom*. Also, the attire which appears on the folding screen, "Jongmyochinjegyujedoseol," shows the use of *namjuui* as well, and the attire in *Siyongmubo* is similar to this.

Figure 53. Attire for *Jeongdaeeop* dancers in *Jongmyouigwe*

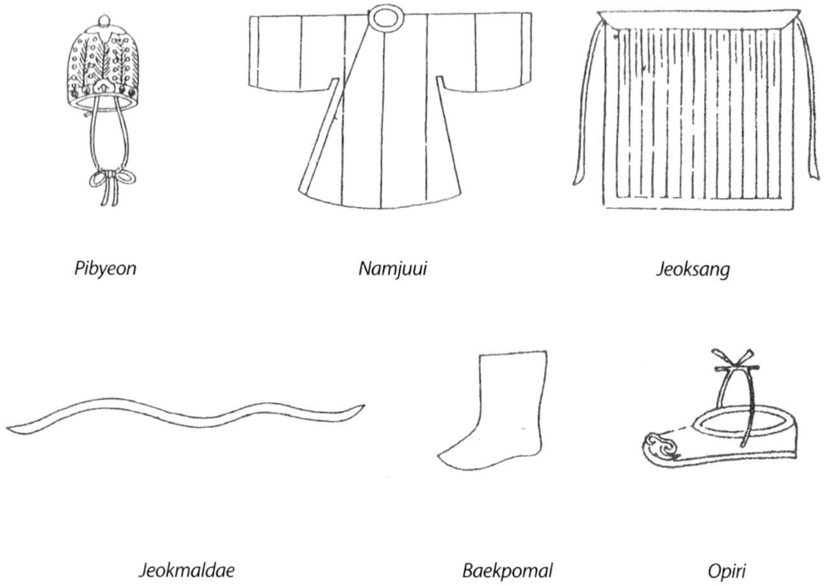

Figure 54. *Mumu* attire in "Jongmyochinjegyujedoseol" (left)
Figure 55. *Mumu* attire in *Siyongmubo* (right)

3) From the Korean Empire to the Present

In the founding year of the Korean Empire (1897), as recorded in *Joseonakgaeyo*, the costume of *ilmu* dancers in *Jeongdaeeop* comprised *bokdu*, *hongjuui*, and *namsadae*, identical to that for *Botaepyeong*. Thus, during the years of the Empire, not only did dancers and musicians share the same attire, but also *Botaepyeong* and *Jeongdaeeop* dancers. This is what has been inherited today for dance attire. Even up to the time of *Chungwantonggo* (1788), shoes for dancers consisted of *opiri*; today, they wear long boots.

Figure 56. Current *munu* attire for *Jongmyo jeryeak*

5. Implements

Traditionally, in *Botaepyeong*, *yak* and *jeok* were used as dance implements, while sword, spear, bow and arrow were used in *Jeongdaeeop ilmu*. Today, this tradition is maintained for *Botaepyeong*. However, in the case of *Jeongdaeeop*, only sword and spear are in use, while the bow and arrow have been discarded. Since little change is observable for *Botaepyeong*, we shall focus on the sword and spear used for *Jeongdaeeop*. The manufacturing method of the sword and spear is well–described in *Akhakgwebeom*.

> The sword is made of wood. The blade is wrapped with silver foil, and the hilt with fish skin. The end of the hilt and the top section of the hilt, where the hilt meets the blade, are gilded. Red and green tassels are attached as ribbons. For those used in ancestral rituals, no gold or silver is used and no color is added.[1]

Since *Botaepyeong* was used for both rituals and banquets at the time of *Akhakgwebeom*, sword ornament was distinguished depending on the occasion. As explained here, the ritual sword is made of wood but had no color or ornaments; however, since no other explanation is given for the ribbon, we can assume that the same red ribbon with green tassel was used here, too.

1) "Jeongdaeeop jeongjae uimuldoseol," in *Akhakgwebeom* Vol. 8

The spear is made of wood. The lower bottom of the red handle is decorated with deer horn. The blade is wrapped with silver foil, to which *sangmo*(象毛, red feather ornament) that looks like *duk* is attached. For that used in ritual, instead of using foil, it is powdered and the end of the hilt is adorned with iron.[2)]

This excerpt describes how the spear used in *ilmu* for *Jeongdaeeop* in *Jongmyo jerye* should differ from the spear used in *Jeongdaeeop* for indigenous court dance, in that the one used in ritual should be powdered and the lower part of handle decorated with iron. Since no explanation is given on the handle itself and the *sangmo*, we should assume that these were identical to those used in banquets.

Such ritual implements, which we might call *Akhakgwebeom*–type implements, were transmitted until the time of *Chungwantonggo*. However, dancers came to use swords and spears similar to those for *dukje* (纛祭, ritual offered to the flag used in the military and in royal processions). The first record of such usage appears in *Joseonakgaeyo*. The sword, in this case, was made of wood, and painted blue, and the spear was also made of wood painted red, and had a powdered blade.[3)] At present, we are using those swords as described in *Akhakgwebeom*.

2) *Ibid*.

3) *Ibid*.

Figure 57. Figures of *geom* and *chang*

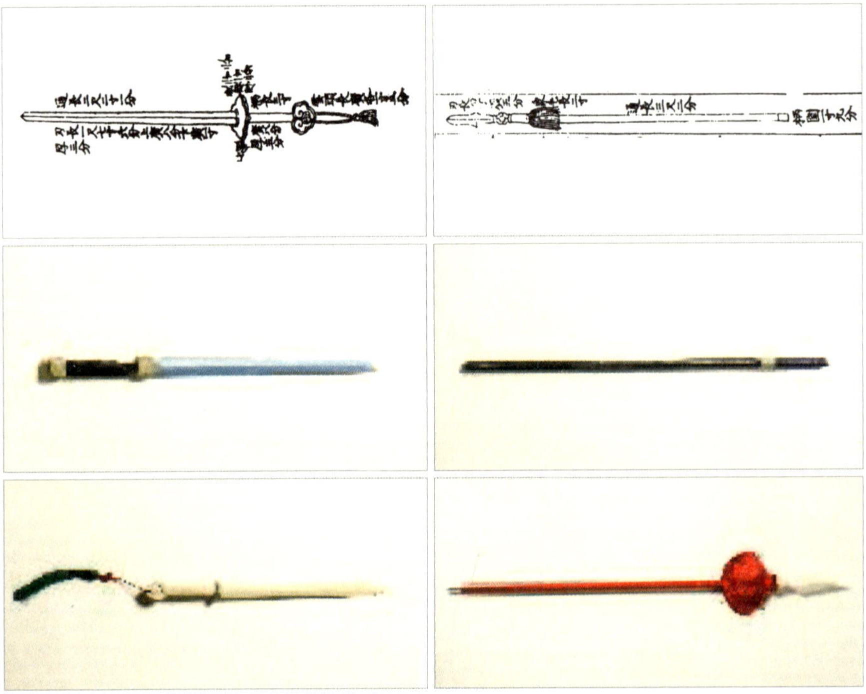

1	2
3	4
5	6

1 *Geom* in *Akhakgwebeom*

2 *Chang* in *Akhakgwebeom*

3 *Geom* used until 2005

4 *Chang* used until 2005

5 *Geom* newly-produced by the National Gugak Center

6 *Chang* newly-produced by the National Gugak Center

Contemporary Transmission of *Jongmyo jeryeak*: Designation as a Cultural Heritage

Contemporary Transmission of *Jongmyo jeryeak* : Designation as a Cultural Heritage

The *Jongmyo jeryeak* that we hear and see today has been transmitted for about 545 years as of 2008, and was created based on *Botaepyeong* and *Jeongdaeeop*, which had been designated as court banquet music at the time of King Sejong. Both *Botaepyeong* and *Jeongdaeeop* were created based on *hyangak* and processional music of the time, and were used in various court ceremonies in Korean history, although their existence was threatened by political crises such national mourning or the dethronement of King Danjong (端宗, r. 1452–1455). King Sejo, after having succeeded to the throne, ordered the performance of this music at court banquets. Moreover, he said "It is a pity that we do not use these grand melodies for our ancestor ritual," and ordered their inclusion in *Jongmyo jeryeak*. This was in 1463, the ninth year of his reign, when he ordered revision of the two pieces to become ritual music. In the following year, they were performed for the first time as ritual music, in the spring ceremony held on January 14th in the lunar calendar. The performance has been discontinued several times over its history, however. For example, it was stopped completely for ten years after the Byeongjahoran, and barely survived during the Japanese colonial period, until it was completely stopped after Liberation. Subsequently, *Jongmyo jerye* was revived in 1969 and continues today.

It is ironic that a tradition with such a long history should have been stopped after the country was liberated. After Liberation, specialists in many fields had numerous responsibilities in the reestablishment of the nation, and could not afford to pay attention to the revival of *Jongmyo jeryeak*. Then, in 1962, the Office of Cultural Properties[1)] initiated discussion on designation of Intangible Cultural Properties. On the first meeting of the second division of the Committee for Cultural Properties, they discussed designating items in the fields of drama, music, dance, and craft that met the following terms:

1. That which helps us understand the change and development of Korean people's lives;
2. That which has been generated with a long history and contains the characteristics of the time;
3. That which is traditional in form and style;
4. That which has great artistic value;

1) As of 1999, the Office of Cultural Properties was raised to the status of Cultural Heritage Administration.

5. That which has value as data for scholarly research;
6. That which can represent its local characteristics and other idiosyncratic features;
7. That which is threatened with becoming extinct.

In the field of music, fourteen items satisfied these requirements : *jeryeak* (祭禮樂, sacrificial ritual music), *yeollyeak* (宴禮樂, music for court rituals and banquets), *daechwita* (大吹打, military processional music), *gagok* (歌曲, the long lyric song), *gasa* (歌詞, the narrative song), *sijo* (時調, the short lyric song), *changak* (唱樂, or *pansori*, solo epic–narrative song with *buk* accompaniment), *sanjo* (散調, virtuoso solo instrumental music with *janggu* accompaniment), *nongak* (農樂, farmers' band music), *japga* (雜歌, semi–art song between folk and art songs), *minyo* (民謠, folk song), *muak* (巫樂, shaman ritual music), *beompae* (梵唄, Buddhist ritual music), and others. Among these, ritual music was first on the list.

During the second meeting of the Committee, held on May 22 of the same year, the method of recording properties and specific ways of conducting preliminary research, once cultural properties and folk material were designated, were discussed. Specialists in each field were chosen and were asked to research their areas and submit reports for the committee to go over. In the field of music, Seong Gyeong-rin (成慶麟, 1911–2008) and Jang Sa-hun (張師勛, 1916–1991) were commissioned. Through such processes, preliminary research was conducted before the committee searched through lists of possible candidates and the designation of cultural properties.

There was the strong opinion that *Jongmyo jeryeak* should be chosen for consideration, and the move for its designation gained support. The following is the list of reasons that it should be designated as a cultural heritage.[2)]

1. Since 1945, after discontinuing the ancestral ritual, we fear that its music shall soon be lost as well.
2. Although we have old notation, it is very different from the actual music. It is thus imperative that we transcribe the music exactly and record actual performances to preserve it.
3. The value of *Jongmyo jeryeak* as important musical cultural heritage is unquestionable, since it reflects our traditional *hyangak* and *gochwiak* of the past four hundred years since King Sejo's period.

Based on such reasoning, investigation into designating *Jongmyo jeryeak* as an Intangible Cultural Heritage was initiated. The research committee, consisting of Yi Hye–gu (李惠求, 1909–2010), Seong Gyeong–rin, and Jang Sa–hun, began work on May 2, 1964, and continued for four months, until September 20. Yi Hye-gu, in a paper entitled "*Jongmyo jeryeak ui sajeok gochal*" (Historical Research of *Jongmyo jeryeak*), examined *akjang*, music, and orchestrations, while Seong Gyeong–rin, in the paper "*Jongmyo jerye uiju*" (Treatises of *Jongmyo jerye*), studied the ancestors to which the individual shrine chambers were assigned, the musical instruments, and treaties of the

2) Seong Gyeong–rin, and Jang Sa–hun, 1964. "Jongmyo jeryeak," in *Muhyeongmunhwajae josabogoseo*, Vol.3 (Seoul: Munhwajae gwalliguk).

ritual. Finally, Jang Sa–hun, in his paper "*Jongmyo jeryeak* : *Botaepyeong* and *Jeongdaeeop*," examined the background of the creation of *Botaepyeong* and *Jeongdaeeop*, and their notation in *Sejong sillok* and other old sources recorded since *Sejo sillok*, as well as a comparative study of notation. In an appendix, he attached notation of *Jongmyo jeryeak*.

Through such research efforts, *Jongmyo jeryeak* was finally designated as Intangible Cultural Heritage no. 1 on December 7, 1964. The reason for designation given at the time reads :

> *Jongmyo jeryeak*, as a composite art-form of music, singing, and dancing, is a newly-created musical tradition applying the traditional ritual musical culture of north-east Asia into the musical tradition of the Joseon Dynasty. It had been transmitted as the model for realizing the ideal of governing people through music and it can be considered as the quintessence of court music, with a unique musical aesthetics of its own.

When first designated, it was under the category of individual, not group, music. The reason for this was because "the designation was awarded to the holder of arts of *Jongmyo jeryeak*, who has been judged by the committee consisting of specialists in the area to be competently trained to perform and preserve *Jongmyo jeryeak* in its authentic and original form." Thus, although *Jongmyo jeryeak* had been acknowledged as an individual art, it is essentially a group art, for which many people must gather to perform properly. As a result, a Preservation Committee for *Jongmyo jeryeak* was formed, and on

February 15, 2001, the Committee was designated as a cultural heritage and group holder of traditional arts. The system of designating a group as cultural heritage is applicable in cases where "the nature of cultural heritage requires that more than one individual is needed in order to perform the given arts." In 2001, Seong Gyeong-rin became the first president of the committee, and, following his death in 2007, Choe Chung-ung, a senior member of the National Gugak Center, succeeded in the position, to become the second president in charge.

| Glossary |

Aak 雅樂 | Literally, "elegant music,"referring to sacrificial ritual music in which melodies from the sacrificial rites of Song China are performed

Aakryeong 雅樂令 | Head musician

Aheon 亞獻 | Second wine offering

Aheongwan 亞獻官 | Officiant in charge of the second wine offering

Aheon–rye 亞獻禮 | The procedure of the second wine offering

Ajaeng 牙箏 | A bowed zither

Ak 樂 | Generally, *ak* refers to music. In *Jongmyo jeryeak*, the meaning of *ak* in its broad sense incorporates instrumental music (*ak*), song (*ga*), and dance (*mu*), while, in its narrow sense, *ak* indicates only instrumental music.

Akgong 樂工 | A court musician

Akhakdogam 樂學都監 | A governmental office of music study

Akhakgwebeom 樂學軌範, | *Guide to the Study of Music*, published in 1493

Akhakjejo 樂學提調 | A high–ranking position in the music bureau

Akjak 樂作 | The beginning of music

Akjang 樂章 | Texts or hymns sung in the ritual with instrumental accompaniment

Akjangyoram 樂章要覽 | An anonymous script containing *gayageum* and *geomungo* parts in *Jongmyo jeryeak*, published before 1829

Akji 樂止 | The ending of music

Akmu 樂舞 | A type of dance performed as *aak* in the Chinese Zhou Dynasty

Aksa 樂師 | Leader of the *akgong* or the *aksaeng*, usually a senior musician

Aksaeng 樂生 | Court musicians in charge of *aak*

Akseo 樂書 | *Treatise on Music*, an ancient Chinese book

Alja 謁者 | An officiant in charge of leading the priests in the ritual

Baehyanggongsin heonggwan 配享功臣獻官 | An officiant in charge of offerings to royal retainers whose tablets were enshrined in Jongmyo

Baejegwan 陪祭官 | Officials participating in the ritual as general officiants, not priests

Baekchodae 白綃帶 | A belt for the formal robe for musicians

Baekgi 白旗 | A white flag; one of the *Osaekgi*

Baekhogi 白虎旗 | Flag of the white tiger

Baekjujungdan 白紬中單 | A white silk inner robe for musicians

Baekjumaldae 白紬抹帶 | A belt for the musicians' attire

Baekpomal 白布襪 | White socks

Bak 拍 | A wooden clapper

Banghyang 方響 | A set of sixteen iron chimes

Beompae 梵唄 | Buddhist ritual music

Bi 匕 | A ceremonial spoon

Biransam 緋鸞衫 | A red silk robe for musicians

Bokdu 幞頭 | A square–shaped flat top hat for government officials

Bongjogwan 捧俎官 | An officiant in charge of carrying the sacrifices

Botaehwa 保太和 | Changed name of *Botaepyeong* during the Japanese colonial period

Botaepyeong 保太平 | A musical suite used in *Jongmyo jerye* consisting of eleven pieces representing the civil achievements of the ancestors

Botaepyeongjiak 保太平之樂 | Referring to the music of *Botaepyeong*

Botaepyeongjimu 保太平之舞 | Referring to *munmu*, civil dance, in *Jongmyo jerye*

Bujitongrye 副知通禮 | An officiant assigned to assist the crown prince

Bunung 奮雄 | The sixth piece of the *Jeongdaeeop* suite

Byeon or Byeongi 籩 or 籩器 | Ceremonial utensils made of bamboo

Byeona 邊兒 | The outer rim of *gaejeok*

Byeongjahoran 丙子胡亂 | Manchu invasion of Korea in 1636

Chang 槍 | A spear

Changak 唱樂 | Solo epic–narrative song with *buk* accompaniment; also called *pansori*

Chanin 贊引 | An official in charge of supervising the order of the ritual

Cheok 戚 | An ax

Cheolbyeondu 徹籩豆 | The procedure of removing the food offering

Cheonggi 青旗 | A blue flag; one of the *Osaekgi*

Cheonghwangjonggung pyeongjo 淸黃鐘宮平調 | *Pyeongjo* mode with Hwangjong in the higher octave as a central tone

Cheongnyeonggi 青龍旗 | Flag of the blue dragon

Cheongsam 青衫 | Lit.,"blue robe,"the musician's attire used in *Jongmyo jerye* from the Korean Empire to the present

Cheonjogwan 薦俎官 | An officiant in charge of presenting the sacrificial meats

Cheonjo–rye 薦俎禮 | The procedure offering the sacrifices

Chijae 致齋 | The last three days of Jaegye, the seven–day purification period prior to the *Jongmyo jerye*

Chilsaheongwan 七祀獻官 | An officiant in charge of offerings to seven gods concerning the people's life

Chingha 稱賀 | The procedure for celebrating the successful completion of the ritual

Chisagwan 致詞官 | An officiant in charge of delivering appreciation

Choheon 初獻 | First wine offering

Choheon–rye 初獻禮 | The procedure of the first wine offering

Chongyu 寵綏 | The eighth piece of the *Jeongdaeeop* suite

Chuk 柷 | A wooden box with a beater

Chuksa 祝史 | An official in charge of the ritual

Chungwan 春官 | *Rites Officials*, a section of *Jurye*

Chungwantonggo 春官通考 | *Code of Courtesy for All Rituals*, published around the time of King Jeongjo

Daeakhubo 大樂後譜 | A book of music from King Sejo's time, compiled in 1759

Daechuk 大祝 | An officiant in charge of reading the prayer

Daechwita 大吹打 | Military processional music

Daeduk 大纛 | A large flag

Daegak 大角 | A large horn

Daegang 大綱 | Groups of *jeonggan*

Daegeum 大笒 | A large transverse bamboo flute

Daegeum or Jing 大金 | A large gong

Daegeumsipcha 大金十次 | Beating the large gong ten times in Jongheon

Daego 大鼓 | A large drum

Daehanyejeon 大韓禮典 | *Code of Courtesy of the Korean Empire*, published in the late 19th century

Daeryeo 大呂 | Name of the second note in the twelve half–step scale

Daesa 大祀 | Large–scale state rituals

Daeseongaak 大晟雅樂 | Court ritual music of the Chinese Song Dynasty, imported to the Goryeo Dynasty court in the early 12th century

Daeseongakbo 大晟樂譜 | A collection of *aak* compiled by Im U during the Chinese Yuan Dynasty

Daeyu 大猷 | The tenth piece of the *Botaepyeong* suite

Dangak 唐樂 | Lit., "music of Tang China," referring not only to the Tang Chinese music imported during the Unified Silla and Goryeo periods, but also to the court music of Song China, excluding *aak*, the sacrificial ritual music

Dangbipa 唐琵琶 | A lute as used in *dangak*

Dangha 堂下 | The courtyard ground where the *heonga* ensemble is located

Dangjeok 唐笛 | A flute as used in *dangak*

Dangpiri 唐觱篥 | An oboe as used in *dangak*

Dangsang 堂上 **|** The high terrace where the *deungga* ensemble is located

Danjong 端宗 **|** Sixth king (r. 1452–1455) of the Joseon Dynasty

Deungga 登歌 **|** An ensemble performing on the terrace of the Jongmyo shrine

Dochang 導唱 **|** A lead singer

Dojo 度祖 **|** Grandfather of King Taejo

Dokgyeong 篤慶 **|** The second piece of the *Jeongdaeeop* suite

Du or Dugi 豆 or 豆器 **|** Ceremonial utensil made of wood

Duk 纛 **|** A flag

Dukje 纛祭 **|** Ritual offered to the flag used in the military and in royal processions

Eo 敔 **|** A tiger–shaped scraper

Eodo 御道 **|** Lit., "the king's way," located in the middle of the second, third, and fourth rows in the configuration of the *deungga* ensemble

Eum 音 **|** Music notes

Eum or yin 陰 **|** Referring to one of the two opposing forces in the Chinese philosophy of *Yin* and *Yang*

Eumbogwi 飮福位 **|** The place for partaking of sacrificial food and drink

Eumboksujo 飮福受胙 **|** A procedure taking place after the third wine offering, in which the Cheonjogwan ritually eats and drinks the food offered to the spirits

Eumnyeo 陰呂 **|** Lit., "*yin* pitch," the even–number notes of the twelve half–step scale

Eumyang ohaengnon 陰陽五行論 **|** Theory of *Yin* and *Yang*, and the Five Elements

Eungjong 應鍾 **|** Name of the twelfth note of the twelve half–step scale

Ga 歌 **|** Songs

Gaejeok 介幘 **|** A headband used by musicians participating in the ritual

Gagok 歌曲 **|** Long lyric song

Gak 角 **|** A horn

Gakdae 角帶 **|** A belt for government officials, also used by musicians performing *Jongmyo jeryeak* today

Gamchal 監察 **|** An official in charge of slaughtering the sacrifices

Gancheok–umo 干戚羽旄 **|** Lit., "*gan*," "*cheok*," and "*umo*" mean a shield, an ax, and feathers, respectively; together, however, they metaphorically refer to "dance"

Gangsinak 降神樂 **|** Music for calling the gods

Gasa 歌詞 **|** Narrative song

Gayageum 伽倻琴 **|** A twelve–string zither

Geogachulgung 車駕出宮 **|** The king's procession from the palace to Jongmyo shrine

Geogahwangung 車駕還宮 **|** The king's return to the palace from Jongmyo shrine

Geohwi 擧麾 **|** Lit., "Hold up the flag," signaling the beginning of music

Geom 劍 **|** A sword

Geomungo or hyeongeum 玄琴 **|** A six–string zither

Geum 琴 **|** A seven–string zither

Geum 金 **|** A gong

Geunjeongjeon 勤政殿 **|** The throne hall in Gyeongbok Palace

Gihwanghu 奇皇后 **|** Empress Gi (Ki), originally from Goryeo, who became empress of Huizing (1320–1370) in the Chinese Yuan Dynasty

Gilrye 吉禮 **|** Lit., "auspicious rites," one of five official ritual categories set by the state

Go 鼓 **|** A drum

Gochuksamseong 鼓柷三聲 **|** Beating the *chuk* three times

Gochwiak 鼓吹樂 **|** Lit., "drumming and blowing" music

Gom 劍 **|** A sword

Gongcheokbo 工尺譜 **|** Simplified–character notation

Gongin 工人 **|** A generic term for court musicians

Goseon 姑洗 **|** Name of the fifth note of the twelve half–step scale

Gukjooryeui 國朝五禮儀 **|** *Code of Courtesy for the Five Rituals*, published in 1474

Gukjooryeui seorye 國朝五禮儀序例 **|** *Reference to the Code of Courtesy for the Five Rituals*, published in

1474

Gungga 宮架 | Different name for the *heonga* ensemble when it is used for an emperor

Gungnipgugagwon 國立國樂院 | National Gugak Center

Gungsi 弓矢 | A bow and arrow

Gungwiryeong 宮闈令 | An official in charge of ancestral tablets

Gwan 管 | A pipe

Gwanchang 灌鬯 | Pouring wine on the ground

Gwanghae-gun 光海君 | Fifteenth king (r. 1609–1623) of the Joseon Dynasty

Gwansewi 盥洗位 | A place for washing hands

Gwesik 饋食 | The procedure of preparing the sacrificial food

Gyeokbagilseong 擊拍一聲 | Striking the *bak* once

Gyeokdobeop 擊挑法 | A playing method especially designed for *gayageum* and *geomungo*

Gyeokgoiltong 擊鼓一通 | Beating the *buk* once

Gyeonghak 經學 | The study of Confucian classics

Gyobanggo 教坊鼓 | A suspended barrel drum

Haegeum 奚琴 | A two-string fiddle

Haphyung 合胸 | The dance posture of holding both hands to the chest and bowing used in *ilmu*

Hawoldae 下月臺 | The courtyard ground of Jongmyo shrine

Heonga 軒架 | An ensemble performing on the ground in the courtyard of the Jongmyo shrine

Heongwan 獻官 | An officiant acts as a priest in the ritual

Heukgi 黑旗 | A black flag; one of the *Osaekgi*

Heukpihwa 黑皮靴 | Black-colored half-boots for government officials in formal attire, worn by musicians performing *Jongmyo jeryeak*

Heunganjiak 興安之樂 | The music played during the procedure for sending off the spirits

Holgi 笏記 | The record of the order of service

Honggi 紅旗 | A red flag, one of the *Osaekgi*

Hongjuui 紅紬衣 | Red robe for musicians

Hongnokcho 紅綠綃 | An ornament of red and green silk cloths used for *jeok*

Huimun 熙文 | The first piece of the *Botaepyeong* suite

Hun 塤 | An ocarina

Hwa 和 | A small mouth organ

Hwanggi 黃旗 | A yellow flag, one of the *Osaekgi*

Hwangjong 黃鐘 | Name of the first note of the twelve half-step scale

Hwangnyonggi 黃龍旗 | Flag of the yellow dragon

Hwanjo 桓祖 | The father (b. 1315–d. 1361) of King Taejo

Hwanjosil 桓祖室 | The chamber for the father of King Taejo in Jongmyo shrine

Hwi 麾 | A flag

Hyangak 鄕樂 | Native Korean music

Hyangbipa 鄕琵琶 | A lute as used in *hyangak*

Hyanggwan 享官 | Officiants serving as priests

Hyangmannyeon 享萬年 | Changed name of *Jeongdaeeop* during the Japanese colonial period

Hyeokjeong 赫整 | The tenth piece of the *Jeongdaeeop* suite

Hyeomnyullang 協律郎 | Officials in charge of the progress of musical performance

Hyeongeum or geomungo 玄琴 | A six-string zither

Hyeongga 亨嘉 | The fourth piece of the *Botaepyeong* suite

Hyeonmi 顯美 | The seventh piece of the *Botaepyeong* suite

Hyeonmu 玄武 | A mystical animal combining the shapes of a turtle and a snake

Hyeonmugi 玄武旗 | Flag of the *hyeonmu*

Hyeopjong 夾鐘 | Name of the fourth note of the twelve half-step scale

Hyungbae 胸背 | Embroidered ornaments in square shape attached to the chest and back of the robe

Ichik 夷則 | Name of the ninth note of the twelve half-step scale

Iilmu 二佾舞 | A type of *ilmu*, four dancers in two lines

Ikjo 翼祖 | Great-grandfather (dates of birth and death unknown) of King Taejo

Ilmu 佾舞 | Lit., "line dance," ritual dance used in *aak*

Imjinwaeran 壬辰倭亂 | The Japanese invasion of Korea in 1592

Imjong 林鐘 | Name of the eighth note of the twelve half–step scale

Iniphuimun 引入熙文 | Referring to the playing of Huimun during the officiants entrance into the chamber

Injo 仁祖 | Sixteenth king (r. 1623–1649) of the Joseon Dynasty

Injo sillok 仁祖實錄 | *The Annals of King Injo*, 50 volumes in 50 books

Inpyeon 仁篇 | Volume 1 of *Sogagwonbo*, music book published in the late Joseon Dynasty

Iui 肄儀 | Learning the customary procedures of the ritual

Jaegye 齋戒 | Purification ceremony

Jaein 宰人 | An official in charge of slaughtering the sacrifices

Jangakwon 掌樂院 | The Royal Music Institute of the Joseon Dynasty

Janggu or Janggo 杖鼓 | A hourglass drum

Japga 雜歌 | Semi–art song between folk and art songs

Jeok 翟 | A dance implement made of pheasant feathers

Jeokmaldae 赤抹帶 | A red belt worn by musicians performing *Jongmyo jeryeak*

Jeoksang 赤裳 | A red skirt worn by *ilmu* dancers

Jeoksangjoyeon 赤裳皂緣 | A red skirt biased with black cloth worn by musicians and *ilmu* dancers

Jeolgo 節鼓 | A barrel drum

Jeolgosamtong 節鼓三通 | Beating the *jeolgo* three times

Jeonak 典樂 | Officials belonging to Jangakwon

Jeong 旌 | A flag adorned with feathers

Jeongdaeeop 定大業 | A musical suite used in *Jongmyo jerye* consisting of eleven pieces representing the military achievements of the ancestors

Jeongdaeeopjiak 定大業之樂 | Referring to the music of *Jeongdaeeop*

Jeongdaeeopjimu 定大業之舞 | Referring to *mumu*, military dance of *Jongmyo jerye*

Jeonggan 井間 | A set of squares representing a rhythmic unit

Jeongganbo 井間譜 | Korean mensural notation

Jeongjeon 正殿 | The main shrine of Jongmyo

Jeongjo 正祖 | Twenty-second king (r. 1776–1800) of the Joseon Dynasty

Jeongmyeong 貞明 | Name of the second half of "Yonggwang–Jeongmyeong," the eighth piece of the current *Botaepyeong* suite, which became a combined piece of "Yonggwang" and "Jeongmyeong" in 1765

Jeongno 正路 | The main road of the courtyard in Jongmyo shrine

Jeongse 靖世 | The ninth piece of the *Jeongdaeeop* suite

Jeonpye 奠幣 | The procedure of gift offering

Jeonpyehuimun 奠幣熙文 | Referring to the playing of Huimun during the Jeonpye–rye; although the melody line is the same as that of Yeongsinhuimun, Jeonpyehuimun is much slower

Jeonsagwan 典祀官 | An official charged with necessary chores for the ritual

Jeonseolsa 典設司 | An office charged with the preparation of tents

Jeryeak 祭禮樂 | Sacrificial ritual music

Jeungbomunheonbigo 增補文獻備考 | *Expanded Edition of the Korean Encyclopedia of Documents and Institutions*, 250 volumes, published from 1903 to 1908

Ji 篪 | A transverse flute

Jimnyeong 輯寧 | The fifth piece of the *Botaepyeong* suite

Jinchan 進饌 | The procedure for food offerings

Jinchanak 進饌樂 | Music pieces used in Jinchan

Jingo 晉鼓 | A large barrel drum

Jingor Daegeum 大金 | A large gong

Jingosamtong 晉鼓三通 | Beating *jingo* three times

Jingosiptong 晉鼓十通 | Beating *jingo* ten times

Jinhyeongwan 進賢冠 | Formal hat for government officials

Jinpungjeong 進豊呈 | Large–scale court banquets for joyful occasions

Jinpyechanjakgwan 進幣瓚爵官 | An officiant in charge of wine and gift offering

Jinseol 陳設 | Setting of offering tables

Jipbagaksa 執拍樂師 | Leading musician in charge of playing *bak*

Jiprye 執禮 | An officiant in charge of reading *holgi*

Jipsaaksa 執事樂師 | Leader of the musicians

Jo 俎 | Lit., "cutting board," a small ceremonial tray

Jongheon 終獻 | Third wine offering

Jongheongwan 終獻官 | Officiant in charge of the third wine offering

Jongheon–rye 終獻禮 | The procedure of the third wine offering

Jongmyo jerye 宗廟祭禮 | The royal ancestral ritual

Jongmyochinjegyujedoseol 宗廟親祭規制圖說 | Referring to a folding screen by this name

Jongmyoryeong 宗廟令 | An official in charge of Jongmyo shrine

Jongmyouigwe 宗廟儀軌 | *Code of Courtesy for Jongmyo jerye*, the first 4 books out of total 9 books were published during the time of King Sukjong

Joseonakgaeyo 朝鮮樂概要 | *Summary of the Music of the Joseon Dynasty*, written by Ham Hwa–jin in 1917

Jujakgi 朱雀旗 | Flag of the red phoenix

Junggeum 中笒 | A medium–sized transverse bamboo flute

Junggwang 重光 | The ninth piece of the *Botaepyeong* suite

Junghwaron 中和論 | Theory of harmony

Jungryeo 仲呂 | Name of the sixth note of the twelve half–step scale

Junso 樽所 | A designated place for wine cups

Jurye 周禮 | *The State System of the Zhou Dynasty*, an ancient Chinese book used in Confucianism

Mangnyo 望燎 | The procedure for burning of the written prayers and sacrificial goods

Mangye 望瘞 | The procedure of observing the burial of the gifts and the prayers, changed to Mangnyo in 1757

Mangyewi 望瘞位 | A place to view the burial of wooden prayer holders and general offerings

Miil 未日 | The day of the goat (the eighth day), according to the twelve earthly branches of the Chinese sexagenary cycle

Minyo 民謠 | Folk song

Mohyeolban 毛血槃 | Tray with the fur and blood of the sacrifices

Mokchang 木槍 | A wooden spear

Mokgeom 木劍 | A wooden sword

Mokhwa 木靴 | Half–boot–shaped shoes used in the middle and late periods of the Joseon Dynasty

Mokjo 穆祖 | Great–great–grandfather (b. ?–d.1274) of King Taejo

Mu 舞 | Dance

Muak 巫樂 | Shaman ritual music

Mumu 武舞 | Military dance

Munmu 文舞 | Civil dance

Muyeok 無射 | Name of the eleventh note of the twelve half–step scale

Myeonbok 冕服 | King's formal ritual costume

Myosa 廟司 | An officiant in charge of cleansing the shrine

Na or Nagak 螺 or 螺角 | A conch shell

Nab–il 臘日 | The third *miil* after the winter solstice in the lunar calendar

Namjuui 藍紬衣 | Blue robe worn by *ilmu* dancers

Namryeo 蕤賓 | Name of the seventh note of the twelve half–step scale

Namui 藍衣 | Blue robe worn by *ilmu* dancers

Nando 鑾刀 | A special knife used only in *Jongmyo jerye* for the sacrifices

Nodo 路鼗 | A pellet drum set

Noeumsu 老陰數 | Lit., "aged *yin* number"

Nogo 路鼓 | A suspended drum set

Nokchosam 綠綃衫 | A green–colored robe worn by the clapper holder

Nongak 農樂 | Farmers' band music

Noyangsu 老陽數 | Lit., "aged *yang* number"

Obanggi 五方旗 | Five cardinal point flags

Obangsaek 五方色 **|** Colors of the five cardinal points
Oeumyakbo 五音略譜 **|** Five–tone abridged notation
Ojeongdae 烏鞓帶 **|** A belt for the formal robes of musicians
Okgyeong 玉磬 **|** A set of stone chimes
Onganjiak 雍安之樂 **|** Music in the form of *aak* played during the procedure of removing the food offering
Opiri 烏皮履 **|** Black leather shoes for musicians
Orye 五禮 **|** Five national rituals
Osaekgi 五色旗 **|** Five–colored flags
Palbang 八方 **|** Eight directions
Palgwae 八卦 **|** The eight trigrams for divination
Palpung 八風 **|** Referring to winds from eight directions
Panwi 版位 **|** A designated place for the king to stand
Pareum 八音 **|** Eight sounding materials: metal, stone, string, bamboo, gourd, earth, leather, and wood
Parilmu 八佾舞 **|** A type of *ilmu*, sixty-four dancers in eight lines
Pibyeon 皮弁 **|** A hat made of deerskin
Pilryul 篳篥 **|** An oboe
Pilseon 弼善 **|** An official in charge of educating the crown prince
Punganjiak 豐安之樂 **|** Music in the form of *aak* played in the procedure of food offering
Pyebaek 幣帛 **|** The offered gift
Pyeonjong 編鐘 **|** A set of sixteen bronze bells
Pyeongyeong 編磬 **|** A set of sixteen stone chimes
Saeng 笙 **|** A mouth organ
Saenggap 牲匣 **|** Ceremonial containers
Saengsu 生數 **|** Lit., "living number"
Sailmu 四佾舞 **|** A type of *ilmu*, sixteen dancers in four lines
Sajikdan 社稷壇 **|** The national altar to the gods of land and grain
Sambangbae 三方拜 **|** Lit., "three–direction bowing," dance used for *Jongmyo jerye* during the Japanese occupation period
Samjaeron or Samjae philosophy 三才論 **|** Theory of Three Principals: heaven, earth, and man as the principle elements of the cosmos in Confucianism
Samjuk 三竹 **|** Lit., "three bamboo," indicating large–, medium–, and small–sized transverse flutes
Sangmo 象毛 **|** Red feather ornament
Sangwoldae 上月臺 **|** The high terrace of Jongmyo shrine
Sanjae 散齋 **|** The first four days of Jaegye, the seven–day purification period prior to *Jongmyo jerye*
Sanjo 散調 **|** Virtuoso solo instrumental music with *janggu* accompaniment
Sanseong byeolgam 山城別監 **|** An official charged with protecting a mountain fortress during the Goryeo period
Sasin 四神 **|** The guards of the four directions
Sejo 世祖 **|** Seventh king (r. 1455–1468) of the Joseon Dynasty
Sejo sillok 世祖實錄 **|** *The Annals of King Sejo*, 49 volumes in 18 books
Sejong 世宗 **|** Fourth king (r. 1418–1450) of the Joseon Dynasty
Sejong sillok 世宗實錄 **|** *The Annals of King Sejong*, 163 volumes in 154 books
Sejongsil 世宗室 **|** The chamber for King Sejong in Jongmyo shrine
Seokjeonakbo 釋奠樂譜 **|** *Confucius Shrine Ritual Notation*, an *aak* music book written by Im U of the Chinese Yuan Dynasty
Seong 成 **|** Lit., "achieve," an unit for counting musical pieces
Seong 聲 **|** Sound
Seongjong 成宗 **|** Ninth king (r. 1469–1494) of the Joseon Dynasty
Seongnihak 性理學 **|** Neo–Confucianism
Seongsaenggi 省牲器 **|** The procedure for examining sacrifices and utensils
Seonjo 宣祖 **|** Fourteenth king (r. 1567–1608) of the Joseon Dynasty
Seonwi 宣威 **|** The fourth piece of the *Jeongdaeeop* suite

Seul 瑟 | A 25–string zither
Sibiji 十二支 | Twelve Earthly Branches
Sijo 時調 | Short lyric song
Silhak 實學 | Practical Learning
Singwan 晨祼 | Welcoming spirits at dawn
Singwan–rye 晨祼禮 | The procedure welcoming spirits at dawn
Sinjeong 神定 | The fifth piece of the *Jeongdaeeop* suite
Sinpyeon 信篇 | Volumes 6 and 7 of *Sogagwonbo*, music book published in the late Joseon Dynasty
Sipgan 十干 | Ten Heavenly Stems
Siyongmubo 時用舞譜 | *Current Dance Notation*, a dance notation book compiled during the time of King Yeongjo and King Jeongjo
Siyongmuyonghaeje 時用舞譜解題 | *Explanation for Siyongmubo*, written by Yi Ju–hwan in 1956
Socha 小次 | A temporary tent for the king
Sogagwonbo 俗樂源譜 | A seven–volume music book, compiled in five books published in the late Joseon Dynasty
Sogeum 小笒 | A small transverse bamboo flute
Somu 昭武 | The first piece of the *Jeongdaeeop* suite
Somujimu 昭武之舞 | Indicating *mumu*, military dance, performed in *aak* performance during the early Joseon Dynasty
Songsin 送神 | Sending off the spirits
Songsin–rye 送神禮 | The procedure for sending off spirits
Sukjong 肅宗 | Nineteenth king (r. 1674–1720) of the Joseon Dynasty
Suneung 順應 | The seventh piece of the *Jeongdaeeop* suite
Suribujak 述而不作 | A traditional compositional method that applied texts to pre–existing melodies by changing rhythms to fit the new text
Taejo 太祖 | The first king (r. 1392–1398) of the Joseon Dynasty
Taejo sillok 太祖實錄 | *The Annals of King Taejo*, 15 volumes in 3 books
Taejong 太宗 | The third king (r. 1400–1418) of the Joseon Dynasty
Taejong sillok 太宗實錄 | *The Annals of King Taejong*, 36 volumes in 16 books
Taejongsil 太宗室 | The chamber for King Taejong in Jongmyo shrine
Taejosil 太祖室 | The chamber for King Taejo in Jongmyo shrine
Taeju 太簇 | Name of the third note of the twelve half–step scale
Taepyeongso 太平簫 | A conical oboe
Takjeong 濯征 | The third piece of the *Jeongdaeeop* suite
Teukgyeong 特磬 | A single stone chime
Teukjong 特鐘 | A single bronze bell
Tungso 洞簫 | A vertical flute
U 竽 | A large mouth organ
Uiin 依仁 | The third piece of the *Botaepyeong* suite during the time of King Sejong
Uijang 儀仗 | Implement holders
Uijeongbu 議政府 | The highest administrative agency of the Joseon Dynasty
Ulchangju 鬱鬯酒 | Wine made of turmeric root
Unmun 雲門 | One of the six kinds of music that deal with the six generations of ancient Chinese emperors or kings; *Unmun* is the music of Hwangje (黃帝)
Uyak 羽籥 | Lit., "*u*" means feathers and "*yak*" refers to a flute, both are used as dance implements
Wolgeum 月琴 | A moon–shaped lute
Wongudan 圜丘壇 | An altar for the rite to the heaven
Yak 籥 | A flute
Yang 陽 | Referring to one of the two opposing forces in the Chinese philosophy of *Yin* and *Yang*
Yanggang 陽剛 | The state of strong *yang*
Yangma 陽亇 | The edged rim between the blade and the hilt of a sword
Yangnoyeon 養老宴 | The feast for elderly people
Yangyul 陽律 | Lit., "*yang* pitch," the odd–number notes of the twelve half–step scale

Ye 禮 | Proper decorum

Yeangnon 禮樂論 | Theory of Rites and Music

Yegi 禮記 | *Classic of Rites* : One of the Five Classics, ancient Chinese books used in Confucianism

Yejo 禮曹 | A branch of the administrative agency responsible for the ritual

Yeokgyeong 易經 | *Classic of Changes*, or *Book of Changes* : One of the Five Classics, ancient Chinese books used in Confucianism

Yeokseong 繹成 | The eleventh piece of the *Botaepyeong* suite

Yeollyeak 宴禮樂 | Music for court rituals and banquets

Yeolmunjimu 烈文之舞 | Indicating *munmu*, civil dance, performed in *aak* performance during the early Joseon Dynasty

Yeonggwan 永觀 | The eleventh piece of the *Jeongdaeeop* suite

Yeongjo 英祖 | Twenty-first king (r. 1724–1776) of the Joseon Dynasty

Yeongnyeongjeon 永寧殿 | The sub–main shrine of Jongmyo

Yeongsin 迎神 | Welcoming spirits

Yeongsinhuimun 迎神熙文 | Referring to the playing of Huimun during the Yeongsin–rye

Yeongsin–rye 迎神禮 | The procedure of welcoming spirits

Yeonsan–gun 燕山君 | Tenth king (r. 1494–1506) of the Joseon Dynasty

Yeuisa 禮儀使 | An officiant in charge of announcing the procedure of the ritual

Yiwangjik aakbo 李王職雅樂譜 | *Court Music Notation of the Yi Royal Family Bureau*, unpublished music score

Yiwangjik aakbu 李王職雅樂部 | Yi Royal Family Bureau of Court Music in the Japanese colonial era

Yongbieocheonga 龍飛御天歌 | Lit., "Songs of the Dragons Flying to Heaven," epic songs composed during the time of King Sejong praising the achievements of the four great ancestors, Mokjo, Ikjo, Dojo, and Hwanjo, and King Taejo and King Taejong

Yonggangbeop 用綱法 | The method of using *daegang*

Yonggwang–Jeongmyeong 龍光貞明 | The eighth piece of the *Botaepyeong* suite

Yubin 蕤賓 | Name of the seventh note of the twelve half–step scale

Yugilmu 六佾舞 | A type of *ilmu*, thirty-six dancers in six lines

Yulja 律字 | Music letter

Yuljabo 律字譜 | Music letter notation

Yunghwa 隆化 | The sixth piece of the *Botaepyeong* suite

Yuso 流蘇 | A tasseled ornament attached to *jeok*

| References |

General

Gungnipgugagwon

2003 *Jongmyojeryeagui jeonseung* [The transmission of Royal Ancestral Shrine ritual music]. Seoul: Gungnipgugagwon.

Jang Sa-hun

1985 *Gugakchongnon* [General introduction to Korean traditional music]. Seoul: *Segwangeumakchulpansa.*

Kim Mun-sik and Song Ji-won

2001 "Gukgajeryeui byeoncheongwa bogwon" [The change and restoration of national rituals]. In *Seoul 20 segi saenghwalmunhwa byeoncheonsa* [History of changes of living culture in 20th century Seoul]. Pyeonjipbu ed. Seoul: Seoulsijeong gaebaryeonguwon.

Seong Gyeong-rin and Jang Sa-hun

1964 "Jongmyo jeryeak." In *Muhyeongmunhwajae josabogoseo je 3 ho* [Investigation report on Intangible Cultural Heritage, Vol. 3]. Seoul: Munhwajaegwalliguk.

Song Ji-won

2001 "Agwongosareul tonghae bon 17 segi jongmyoakjang nonui" [A discussion of the 17th century Jongmyoakjang based on Agwongosa]. *Munheongwa haeseok* vol. 15.

Yi Hye-gu

1985 "Sejongjo eumangmunhwaui hyeondaesajeok jaeinsik" [New understanding of the music culture of King Sejong's period from a contemporary perspective]. In *Hangugeumangnonjip*. Seoul: Segwangeumakchulpansa.

Classics

Akhakgwebeom (樂學軌範)
Bomanjaechongseo (保晩齋叢書)
Chungwantonggo (春官通考)
Daehanyejeon (大韓禮典)
Goryeosa (高麗史)
Gukjooryetongpyeon (國朝五禮通編)
Gukjooryeui (國朝五禮儀)
Gukjooryeui seorye (國朝五禮儀序例)
Jeungbomunheonbigo (增補文獻備考)
Jongmyouigwe (宗廟儀軌)
Joseonwangjosillok (朝鮮王朝實錄)
Jurye (周禮)
Noneojipju (論語集註)
Sejongsillogakbo (世宗實錄樂譜)
Sejosillogakbo (世祖實錄樂譜)
Taesangji (太常誌)
Yegi (禮記)